FamilyFun
Parties

Homemade Party Hats,
Page 18

FamilyFun Parties

By Deanna F. Cook

and the experts at FamilyFun magazine

This book is dedicated to the readers of *FamilyFun* magazine

Most of the parties and photographs in this book were previously published in *FamilyFun* magazine.

FamilyFun magazine is a division of Disney Publishing Worldwide, Inc. To order a subscription, call 800-289-4849.

FamilyFun Magazine

BOOK EDITORS: Deanna F. Cook, Alexandra Kennedy, and Cindy A. Littlefield
MANAGING EDITOR: Priscilla Totten
ART DIRECTOR: David Kendrick
COPY EDITORS: Laura MacKay, Paula Noonan, and Susan Roberts
EDITORIAL ASSISTANTS: Megan Fowlie, Grace Ganssle, Debra Liebson, and Julia Lynch
ART ASSISTANT: Kathryn Ellsworth
PRODUCTION EDITORS: Jennifer Mayer and Martha Jenkins
TECHNOLOGY COORDINATOR: Luke Jaeger
CONTRIBUTING CRAFT DEVELOPER: Maryellen Sullivan

Impress, Inc.

CREATIVE DIRECTOR: Hans Teensma
DESIGNER: Pamela Glaven

The staffs of *FamilyFun* and **Impress, Inc.** conceived and produced *FamilyFun Parties* at 224 Main Street, Northampton, MA 01060

For information address Disney Editions, 114 Fifth Avenue, New York, New York, 10011-5690. Visit www.disneyeditions.com

Printed in Hong Kong

Library of Congress Cataloging-in-Publication Data on file

ISBN: 0-7868-5375-1

First Paperback Edition

10 9 8 7 6 5 4 3 2 1

Acknowledgments

FamilyFun Contributors

Special thanks to the following *FamilyFun* magazine writers for their wonderful party ideas: Barbara Albright, Rani Arbo, Lynne Bertrand, Cynthia Caldwell, Maryellen Kennedy Duckett, Dorothy Foltz-Gray, Linda Guica, Jenifer Harms, Ann Hodgman, Teri Keough, Heidi King, Vivi Manuzza, Shoshana Marchand, Samuel Mead, Maggie Megaw, Charlotte Meryman, Susan Milord, Jean Mitchel, Rebecca Lazear Okrent, Jodi Picoult, Susan Purdy, Barbara Rowley, Jonathan Sapers, Shannon Summers, Emily B. Todd, Michele Urvater, Penny Warner, and Stacey Stolman Webb.

FamilyFun Readers

Special thanks also to the following *FamilyFun* readers who shared the party ideas that have been a success with their families: Maureen Aderman, Eileen Allen, Mary Ann Ammon, Susan Andrews, Darcey Archuleta, Kristin Ballou, Carey Bentson, Connie Bonaccio, Diana Bosworth, Sherry Branch, Janine Calsbeek, Dawne Carlson, Marianne Cashman, Sally Clark, Rhonda Cloos, Donna Conti, Robin Conti, Ellen Costigan, Karla Davison, Amy Diaz, Jill Driscoll, Emily Edgerley, Teresa K. Edminston, Christine Edwards, Mary Ann Eusebio, Dana W. Fiore, Carol Fitzgerald, Jan Foley, Edith Gholson, Janice Graham, Janelle Gray, Christy Hammond, Vicki Hodges, Shirley Hooey, Kim Jaworski, Bee Jones, Mary Margaret Krause, Sharon Lawton, Kathy Lecate, Katie Lemberg, Lauri Levenberg, Lynn Lutz, Mindy Malone, Susan Matthews, Caitlin McCoy, Mandy McMillen, Carrie Melson, Judy Miller, Rachael Muro, Marlene Parmentier, Karla Paterson, Ann C. Petersen, Zee Ann Poerio, Deborah Lee-Quinn, Denise Dahlin Radecke, Patty Rawlison, Rosemary Riccio, Cathy Rickarby, Carol Schmidt, Lindy Schneider, Linda Schrupp, Lisa Shugart, Amy L. Smellie, Kelly Newman Smith, Jane Smith, Elaine V. Snyder, Jan Aldrich Solow, the Trifone family, Patricia Vara, Amanda Walker, the Wallace family, Kellie Weenink, Robin Williams, Terry Wright, and the Yaun family.

FamilyFun Staff

With gratitude to all the staff of *FamilyFun*'s art and editorial departments, who directed much of the original work. In addition to the book staff, we'd like to acknowledge the following staff members: Jonathan Adolph, Douglas Bantz, Deborah Geigis Berry, John Bidwell, Nicole Blasenak, Dawn Chipman, Jean Graham, Ann Hallock, Ginger Barr Heafey, Elaine Kehoe, Ed Kohn, Gregory Lauzon, Mark Mantegna, Catherine McGrady, Dan Mishkind, Mike Trotman, and Sandra L. Wickland.

ABOUT THE EXPERTS AT *FAMILYFUN*:

Deanna F. Cook, Senior Editor of *FamilyFun* magazine, is the editor of *FamilyFun's Cookies for Christmas, FamilyFun's Crafts,* and *FamilyFun's Cookbook,* all from Hyperion, and the author of *The Kids' Multicultural Cookbook* and *Kids' Pumpkin Projects* from Williamson. She lives in Northampton, Massachusetts, with her husband, Doug, and her party-loving daughter, Ella Skye.

Alexandra Kennedy is the Editorial Director of *FamilyFun* magazine and *Disney Magazine.* She and her husband, James Haug, throw parties in Northampton, Massachusetts, with their two sons, Jack and Nicky.

Cindy A. Littlefield, Associate Editor of *FamilyFun* magazine, lives in Conway, Massachusetts, with her two kids, Ian and Jade, who never pass up an opportunity to celebrate with friends and relatives.

Special thanks to all the photographers, stylists, and models for their excellent work, which first appeared in *FamilyFun* magazine.

This book would not have been possible without the staff at Hyperion, especially Bob Miller, Wendy Lefkon, Richard Thomas, Vincent Stanley, and David Lott.

Contents

Ice-Cream Clown Cone, page 61

Barnyard Invitation, page 25

Mermaid Party Favors, page 45

Cool-Off Party, page 101

Ladybug Party Plate, page 56

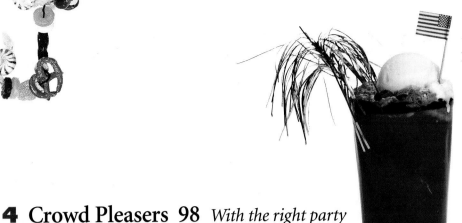

Party Decorations, page 13

Chapter One

Planning a Party

Invitations ★ Decorations
Food ★ Games ★ Crafts ★ Activities
Etiquette ★ Favors & Prizes

D OGGIE!" was my daughter Ella's first word — and first true passion in life. At 12 months, she would pant like a dog, put out a paw, and crawl after her four-legged friends, much to the surprise of her not-so-dog-inclined mom. So for her first birthday, my husband and I threw her a simplified version of the puppy party on page 50. She screeched with delight at the cardboard doghouse and devoured the dalmatian cake with peppermint patty spots. I knew on that day we had a party animal on our hands, and that this was the first of many parties we would throw for her — and with her.

Parties, after all, are a part of a happy childhood. And despite the work and cost of planning them, they're a heck of a lot of fun for parents, too. Getting together with friends for birthdays, holidays, or even a simple dinner party helps mark the all-too-fast-moving years of childhood. And the best parties become an annual tradition.

At *FamilyFun* magazine, we know how important it is for every party to be a hit. Through the years, our readers, parents with kids ages three to 12, have come to depend on our party plans, whether they're for a slumber birthday bash, summer cool-off fest, neighborhood potluck, or block party. The plans we print are complete, from the invitations to the cake to the thank-you notes, and they are always tested out by families.

In this book, you'll find the best parties from *FamilyFun* magazine. Like Ella's first birthday, I hope the celebrations that this book inspires go down in your own family fun history.

— *Deanna F. Cook*

Party Planning

Party Worksheet

Once you have settled on a party in this book, copy the following list onto a large piece of paper and use it to track decisions about the party. Keep a shopping list running simultaneously.

✓ **Theme:**
✓ **Location:**
✓ **Date:**
✓ **Time:**
✓ **Guests:**
✓ **Prizes and favors:**
✓ **Helpers:**
✓ **Invitations:**
✓ **Decorations:**
✓ **Menu:**
✓ **Games:**
✓ **Crafts:**
✓ **Activities:**
✓ **Supplies:**

THROWING a successful party need not be expensive or exhausting — and the memories it will create can last a lifetime. Simple planning and family teamwork are the key. Invite your child to flip through the pages of this book to find a plan, then take a close look at the Party Stats (in the balloons) to make sure it fits your budget, works within your time frame, and is age appropriate. Here are some basic planning tips to get you in the party spirit.

Allow time for planning: A great birthday or block party can take as long as a month to plan at a non-stressful pace. Other parties, such as those featured in the "Everyday Parties" chapter on page 74, can be planned and executed in a day. Be sure to allow time for setting up (use our estimated prep time as a guideline).

Enlist help: Ask your spouse, a neighbor, an older child, a relative, or a baby-sitter for support both for the planning and for the party. Of course, all during the planning stage, be sure to include your kids, who will have lots of ideas.

Pick a theme: Parties are fun when they revolve around a child's current passion or a family's personal interest, from ballerinas to beaches. A theme also helps spark your imagination when it comes to invitations, decorations, food, favors, and games. Suggest the theme and go over ideas with your family (to make sure no one has moved on to a new one). At the same time, not every party has to have a theme. You can mix and match games, invitations, and crafts from any of our plans for a successful party.

Choose an age-appropriate party: We have recommended an age range for each party, but don't let that number restrict you. For instance, if your eight-year-old would rather throw a doll's tea party than a mermaid bash, adapt a birthday party to suit her interests and abilities.

Settle on a budget that suits your family: In each party, we estimated the cost per guest, assuming three favors each would be plenty.

Use this figure as a starting point — if you feel like spending more, splurge on every favor on the list; if the estimate seems too steep, trim away. The easiest way to hold down costs is to make as much as you can, from the invitations to the decorations, favors, and food.

Choose a location: Home parties, either inside or in the backyard, are nice for any age and definitely work best for children ages four and under. Outdoor locales, whether a backyard or a skating rink, have the advantage of space and spare your house wear and tear. Still, it may be harder to control the boundaries, and events depend on Mother Nature. For more location ideas, see page 214.

Set a time limit: For birthday parties, a few hours of playing games, eating cake, and opening presents is plenty. Family parties, on the other hand, tend to have a looser schedule and can last an entire afternoon. When determining the length of a party, keep in mind your child's (or family's) energy level and plan accordingly.

Structure the party: Think of a party as consisting of segments: the welcoming activity, the games, the refreshments, and the closing activity. As guests arrive, plan an icebreaking activity, such as making party hats, for them to do until everyone shows up. When all guests are present, open with a game that lets the entire group interact. Thereafter, change the pace so that boisterous games are followed by calmer ones. Make the last game before refreshments a calm one and plan free play for the farewell activity.

Go with the flow: Once the party is in full swing, don't be afraid to repeat a game that was a huge hit — or scratch one you think won't go over well now that you know the mood of the party. The most important thing is to plan a structure before the party, then remain as flexible as possible once it is under way. Once you've settled on an order, write it down and use it only as a guideline. If something doesn't go as planned, roll with the punches and change activities, and your party will be a winner.

Memory Makers

Capture the spirit of your party on film with these photo tips:

☛ Before the party, make sure your camera battery and flash are working.

☛ Assign a roaming photographer, such as Dad, a sitter, or a teenage sibling, to take pictures.

☛ Turn party guests into photographers by passing out disposable cameras.

☛ Set up a photo backdrop for posing guests (see page 29).

☛ Assemble all your party shots into a mini album as a keepsake.

☛ If you own or can borrow a video camera, film the party highlights.

☛ Be candid — too many posed shots may dampen the fun.

Party Invitations

Creative Invitations

☞ **For a plane or train party, send "tickets" with boarding passes.**
☞ **Write the invitations on balloons, puzzles, paper chains, or the back of photos.**
☞ **Make one master invitation (a child's drawing, a collage, or a computer design) and photocopy it.**
☞ **Send a musical invitation — a cassette with theme music.**
☞ **Decorate the envelope with stickers to fit the theme.**
☞ **Deliver invitations dressed in a costume that relates to the party theme.**
☞ **Stuff the card with glitter or confetti.**

SOME PARTIES, such as a special dinner for grandparents, might not call for invitations. A phone call or e-mail will do. Most parties, though, benefit from a written invitation. They set the tone for a party, establish the theme, and excite guests to come. Before sending out your invitations, review the designs we feature with each party plan, as well as the following hints.

Start with the guest list: When making the guest list, consider the size of your house (or yard) and how many guests you can comfortably manage. If you're throwing a children's party, you can use the old formula that the child's age determines the number of attendees (a five-year-old would invite five friends, for example), but if you think you can handle the entire class, by all means, do so.

Include party particulars: On your invitation, list who the party is for, what the theme is (if any), and where the party will be located (along with directions, if necessary). You'll also want to include both the starting and ending times so parents know when to pick their kids up.

List special instructions: It's a good idea to mention if a meal will be served or if it's simply cake and ice cream. You should also list any items guests should bring along, such as a swimsuit for a pool party.

Request an RSVP: Include your phone number and a date you'd like a response by. When parents call to RSVP, ask if they plan on staying and if their child has any food allergies or conditions, such as asthma. For larger parties, write "regrets only."

Send invitations at least two weeks in advance: This allows guests plenty of time to respond while giving you the chance to finalize the amount of food or favors you need.

Party Decorations

PARTY CALLS for a festive atmosphere, so go ahead and dress up your space with balloons and streamers. For ideas, you may want to hit a party supply store (for resources, see page 214), but don't overdo it. When it comes to decorations, a little goes a long way, especially for younger kids.

Set up the space: A party is a good excuse to clean house, enlisting help, of course, as needed. In the room where games will be played, pack away any breakables and clear the furniture, too.

Hang balloons and streamers: Nothing says "it's a party" more than balloons and streamers. Choose colors that match your theme, such as orange and black for a Halloween bash or blue and green for a mermaid party. Hang them in the party room — and on the mailbox, too. Note: For preschoolers, purchase Mylar balloons (latex balloons are a choking hazard).

Turn toys into props: To keep costs down, dress up the party room with props you already own, strategically placed. Place a red wagon of stuffed animals on the porch for a farm party; hang a sombrero in the dining room for a Mexican fiesta.

Handcraft decorations: Paper chains, banners, and signs are simple decorations kids can make the week before the party.

Spiff up the table: Start with a colorful tablecloth, cups, and novelty plates (use paper for easy cleanup). Then get creative with napkin folding, centerpieces, and handcrafted place cards.

Think all-natural: For low-cost charm, spruce up your house with seasonal finds. Try a vase of spring tulips at an Easter party, pine boughs for a Christmas bash, or pumpkins and Indian corn at a fall festival.

Birthday Throne

FamilyFun contributor Pamela Glaven of South Deerfield, Massachusetts, found a novel way to make the birthday child or guest of honor feel like a king or queen. She decorates a special chair with streamers and balloons to look like a throne.

Party Food

The Best Party Cake Ever

If you have enough time to bake a cake from scratch, this classic yellow party cake is the one. It's rich and buttery without being too sweet, and sturdy enough to be cut into all of our cake shapes.

> 3/4 cup unsalted butter, softened
>   to room temperature
> 1½ cups sugar
> 3 large eggs (for a white cake
>   substitute 6 egg whites)
> 3 cups all-purpose flour
> 2 teaspoons baking powder
> 1 teaspoon cream of tartar
> 1⅓ cups buttermilk (or 1 cup
>   buttermilk and ⅓ cup plain
>   yogurt)
> 2½ teaspoons vanilla extract

Preheat the oven to 350°. Butter and lightly flour your cake pans (see our list of pan sizes below). Cream the butter and sugar until light and fluffy. Add the eggs one at a time, beating well after each addition.

Sift together the dry ingredients. Mix the buttermilk, vanilla extract, and butter mixture into the dry ingredients, one third at a time, scraping the bowl frequently. Pour into the prepared pans and bake according to the times listed below, or until a toothpick inserted in the center comes out clean. Serves 10 to 12.

Our Best Party Cake Ever batter can be baked in all sorts of overproof pans and bowls. If you don't already own the pans we suggest for our cake designs, you can buy disposable versions (or borrow them from a neighbor). Pour the batter from one batch of this recipe into any of the following combinations of pans and bake as directed.

☞ Two 8- or 9-inch rounds or squares; bake for 20 to 35 minutes

☞ One 13- by 9- by 2-inch pan; bake for 35 to 40 minutes

☞ Two bundt or ring pans; bake for 20 to 30 minutes

☞ Two 12-cup cupcake tins; bake for 10 to 12 minutes

☞ Two 6-inch half spheres (available at cake supply stores) or two 1½-quart ovenproof bowls (stainless steel or Pyrex); bake for 30 minutes

☞ Two rimmed 12- or 14-inch pizza pans; bake for 20 to 30 minutes

☞ Five mini loaf pans; bake for 20 to 30 minutes

The Icing on the Cake

This classic buttercream icing is quick and easy to prepare and can be flavored in any way the birthday child fancies.

> 1 cup unsalted butter, softened
>   to room temperature
> 3 cups sifted confectioners'
>   sugar
> 2 teaspoons vanilla extract
> 2 tablespoons light corn syrup
> 1 tablespoon milk

In the bowl of an electric mixer, cream the butter until fluffy. Add the remaining ingredients and beat until smooth. Makes 4 cups.

Chocolate Frosting: Substitute ½ to ¾ cup of cocoa powder for an equal amount of confectioners' sugar.

Cream Cheese Frosting: Substitute 4 ounces of cream cheese for ½ cup of butter and use lemon juice instead of the milk. Beat in an additional 1½ to 2 cups confectioners' sugar and omit the light corn syrup.

Strawberry or Raspberry Frosting: Add ¼ cup seedless strawberry or raspberry jam to the basic frosting recipe. Add an additional ½ cup of confectioners' sugar and omit the light corn syrup.

A PARTY JUST isn't a party without good food. When planning your menu, keep things simple and stick with your theme. The following tips, and the recipes listed in each party, will help you prepare foods everyone loves.

Make it familiar: Parties are not the time to introduce new foods to children. Save yourself time (and peace of mind) by preparing the old standbys, such as sandwiches, pizza, tacos, and hot dogs. You can make these foods more impressive by jazzing up the presentation or the name to fit your theme. For instance, use cookie cutters to cut sandwiches into stars for a Fourth of July party; at a puppy party Pigs in a Blanket can be renamed Dachshunds in a Bed.

Serve finger foods: A rule of thumb for feeding crowds is to make everything small — crudités, finger sandwiches, mini fruit kabobs, and bite-size cheese and crackers. If you plan an assortment of, say, six hors d'oeuvres, plan two of each per guest. You may also want to have a big bowl of munchies, such as tortilla chips (and salsa), popcorn, pretzels, or party mix.

Choose dishes that can be made ahead: To spare yourself stress on the day of the party, prepare as much food as you can in advance. Bake and freeze the birthday cake or cut vegetables for crudités.

Balance sweets with nutritious snacks: Because kids tend to load up on too much cake and ice cream, be sure to serve nutritious snacks. Not only will this balance out your menu, but it will keep the games under control, too.

Serve drinks for thirsty guests: Offer guests a drink when they arrive — juice boxes or chocolate milk for a child or party punch for an adult — and keep guests hydrated during party games. To free space in your refrigerator, pack the drinks in coolers with ice.

Don't forget dessert: Behind every memorable party is a great cake. With creative cuts, our Best Party Cake Ever recipe at left can be adapted to fit any party theme.

Planning a Party

Party Games

15 Classic Party Games

- ◆ **Pin the tail on the donkey**
- ◆ **Musical chairs**
- ◆ **Costume relays**
- ◆ **Red light, green light**
- ◆ **Mother, may I?**
- ◆ **Blind man's bluff**
- ◆ **Hide-and-seek**
- ◆ **Hot potato**
- ◆ **Leapfrog**
- ◆ **Red rover**
- ◆ **Spud**
- ◆ **Duck, duck, goose**
- ◆ **Simon says**
- ◆ **Bingo**
- ◆ **Charades**

WHEN ALL is said and done, parties are remembered for the games that made everyone laugh and cheer. Here are some tips for choosing the best ones for your party.

Choose age-appropriate games: Provide the environment for a terrific time by choosing games that work well with the temperaments and ages of the guests. Preschoolers' short attention spans, for instance, mean they can be easily overwhelmed, so simplicity is key. This crowd enjoys duck, duck, goose, pin the tail on the donkey, Simon says, and musical chairs.

School-age kids, on the other hand, like to try new things and can follow more complex rules. Appeal to their sociability, too, with games that call for teamwork, such as Twister, blind man's bluff, and relay races. Preteens enjoy the privileges of getting older and like updated versions of grown-up games, such as name that tune, charades, and trivia games.

Rename classics to fit your theme: Most kids know the rules to the classics — a big advantage for the harried host. Brainstorm with your child to come up with variations, such as pin the patch on the pirate, musical beach towels, splash tag, or fish, fish, shark.

Plan extra games: Plan as many games as you can in case you have misjudged how long they take. Try not to let games go on so long that guests are waiting awkwardly for others to finish (10 minutes is ample time for a game); elimination games, in particular, create this problem. At the same time, allow winners a minute to bask in their glory before moving on to the next game.

Party Piñata

Piñatas are a smashing success at any children's party. Our hot air balloon design is easy to craft, and easy for kids to break. With a little creativity, the balloon can be modified into a dinosaur egg, basketball, or pumpkin.

1. In a bowl, mix up papier-mâché paste. Combine ½ cup flour and 2 cups cold water. Add that mixture to a saucepan of 2 cups boiling water and bring to a boil. Remove from heat and stir in 3 tablespoons sugar. Let cool.

For the base of the balloon, blow up a 14-inch balloon. For stability, place it in a 10-inch bowl. Fold a two-page spread of newspaper in half and then in half again. Tear (don't cut) 1½-inch-wide strips so they have a slightly rough edge. Drag a strip of newspaper through the paste, wipe off any excess, and place it at an angle on the balloon. Place the second strip so that it slightly overlaps the first. Continue until the balloon is covered with one layer, leaving a 2-inch-square hole at the top for adding the candy. Give it 24 hours to dry. Cover your leftover paste with plastic wrap so it doesn't dry out.

2. For the piñata's hanger, wrap the midpoint of a length of string around the bottom of the balloon, pulling the ends up to the top; tape it to the balloon in a few places. Knot together the ends of the string 6 inches above the top. Tape the top half of a 32-ounce yogurt container to the bottom of the balloon (for the hot air balloon neck).

3. Cover the balloon (including the string), the neck, and the bottom half of the yogurt container (which will become the balloon basket) with a layer of strips of comics dipped in papier-mâché. Place the strips at a different angle from the first layer. Allow the second layer to dry.

4. Cover the balloon, neck, and basket with strips of plain newsprint going in a third direction. Smooth over rough edges as you work. Dry thoroughly.

5. Punch four holes into the neck of the hot air balloon and four into the basket. Attach string to the neck to later suspend the basket about 3½ inches from the base of the balloon.

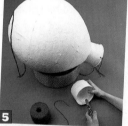

6. Dot the corners of a tissue paper square with a glue stick and place it just to the side of the 2-inch square on the top of the balloon. Follow with other squares in the same color, working your way diagonally down around the balloon. When you get to the bottom, start at the top again in another color to create a houndstooth pattern.

7. Cover the basket with squares of tissue paper. Attach the basket to the balloon. Puncture the uncovered balloon at the top of the piñata and remove all of the balloon fragments. Make sure the inside of the piñata is dry before you fill it, so the candy won't stick to the sides. Fill it about halfway with the candy. Cover the opening with some tissue squares, and it's ready to hang.

Party Crafts

Photo Frames

FamilyFun reader Bee Jones of Poway, California, came up with imaginative favors for her granddaughter's birthday party. As the guests arrived, she took a photo of each one with the birthday girl. Once everyone was there, she also took a group picture. While her daughter ran the party, Bee took the film to a one-hour developer. In the meantime, the children made and decorated Popsicle stick picture frames. When she returned, each guest glued her photo into her frame, and the birthday girl put the group shot into hers. Everyone went home with a special party memory.

WHETHER YOU'RE decorating a baseball hat at a sports party or painting clay pots at a flower party, crafts are often a showstopping activity. They also serve a dual purpose — as a party activity and a take-home favor. Most of the parties in this book feature at least one craft. If you plan on using any of our ideas, review these tips first.

Plan a craft as a welcome activity: Guests typically arrive at different times — and they may not know one another — so ease them into the party with an art project. Invite them to sign in on a newsprint mural, decorated thematically (an empty ocean for a mermaid party or haunted house for a Halloween party). Or, let them craft something to wear at the party, such as hats, headbands, or masks.

Test craft projects before guests arrive: To avoid disappointment, give all art projects a test run. That way, you'll get a sense of how easy the craft is to execute, how long it takes, if it's age appropriate, and most importantly, if it's fun.

Set up a work space: Lay out all the materials for the craft on a low table with comfortable chairs. If it's a messy activity, cover the area with newspaper, or better yet, set up outdoors. Have a few old shirts on hand for kids to wear as cover-ups over their party clothes.

Turn crafts into favors: The best party crafts are keepsakes that remind the guest of the special occasion. Kids ages seven and up enjoy using puffy paint or fabric markers to decorate T-shirts at an art party, pillowcases at a slumber party, or stockings at a Christmas party. Other crafting hits include making jewelry, toys, or photo frames.

Homemade Party Hats

At children's parties, kids love to costume themselves in festive hats, from birthday crowns to princess tiaras to witches' hats. Set out hatmaking supplies, such as construction paper, markers or crayons, glue sticks, sequins, pasta noodles, glitter, buttons, and feathers. Enlist the help of a creative teenager or friend to craft the basic hat shapes to fit, then let guests decorate the wearable art. The hats will instantly put guests into the party spirit.

Party Activities

AMES, CRAFTS, and even cake and ice cream are all highly supervised elements of children's parties. The following activities, on the other hand, relieve the host from directing the party and invite guests to simply enjoy each other's company.

Allow time for free play: At parties, allot time for kids to do what they like best: play. At a construction party, set up toy dump trucks in a sandbox; a backyard cookout calls for Frisbees or a croquet set. Unstructured play time gives kids the freedom for make-believe and impromptu games.

Sing and dance: Background music adds atmosphere to any party, and it may even motivate guests to get up and cut a rug. For a birthday party, play or sing children's songs; at an Italian dinner, crank up Italian opera; and at a Christmas party, gather around the piano for carols.

Watch a show: If you feel like splurging, hire an entertainer, such as a clown, magician, storyteller, or musician (see page 215 for resources). Or, enlist the help of an entertaining friend, such as a teenager who happens to have a few tricks up his sleeve or a dad who plays the accordion.

The Ultimate Treasure Hunt

A treasure hunt is often the favorite event at parties for two reasons: it includes everyone and everyone loves loot. But the real appeal of the hunt (though no hunter would admit this) lies in its delayed gratification. Each new clue brings the search party closer to a prize that the seekers are half hoping they never find. Here are some tips on executing the perfect treasure hunt.

☞ Hunts adapt beautifully to any theme. Instead of being generic, have the clues, the chest, and the treasure relate to the party. For instance, at a bug party, hide plastic ants, gummy worms, and bug stickers in a picnic basket.

☞ Preparation is key. Walk around and note clever places where you could hide clues (the mailbox, a flowerpot, the tire swing).

☞ Start in reverse. Hide the treasure first, picking a spot in your yard or house where you want everyone to end up. Write the clue that will bring kids to this location (it's easier to do this on the spot rather than from another vantage point). Next walk around your yard to find a hiding place for this clue. Right then and there, compose the clue that describes this new place. Repeat this process until you have hidden all your clues.

☞ Write clues that test the seekers' sleuthing abilities ("I once swung people, but now I'm re-tired" is a tire swing). Make a list of each clue and where each is hidden, in case you yourself forget where they're hidden or if one has disappeared and must be read aloud in order to send the seekers on.

☞ Make sure boundaries are well defined, especially outdoors, to keep kids from wandering into restricted areas or all over the house.

☞ Clues can take on many forms — riddles, coded messages, or drawings.

☞ Everyone wins. Whatever is found, whether sought by one group or teams, should be divided evenly and handed out.

Party Etiquette

Giving Thanks

FamilyFun reader Jan Foley of Albany, New York, discovered a creative way to coax her son to write thank-you notes after his birthday parties. She orders double prints of photographs taken during the event, and her son incorporates them into homemade cards. He chooses which photo to include in each note and then pastes it inside colorful paper. Next he writes a brief message. Guests — and their parents — enjoy the photograph sent in a timely fashion.

Another way to show appreciation with pictures is to take a photo of your child wearing or playing with the gift and include it inside the thank-you note sent to the giver. Distant relatives will especially cherish the up-to-date keepsakes.

As any parent knows, children's parties are more than just fun and games. They are one of a child's first introductions to social situations and, as such, raise delicate issues for kids and parents alike. Before your party, give your child a quick briefing on all things mannerly.

Make guests feel welcome: Encourage your child to greet each guest as he arrives, and to see to it, as best as he can, that the guest has a good time during the party. It's also important that the host thank each guest for coming at the end of the party.

Be tactful with invitations: On your child's party guest list, he should include his best friends as well as anyone who might feel left out. Siblings close in age should be invited but discouraged from upstaging the birthday child. If the guest is under five, you can expect him to bring a date, namely his mother.

Let every guest win at least once: If your child wants to play competitive games, try to orchestrate them so that every child wins convincingly at least once. Better yet, plan a few cooperative games, in which the whole gang faces a challenge, such as following a treasure map, then splits the loot evenly.

Accept gifts with a smile: It can take an entire childhood to learn the art of receiving gifts. The receiver should say something nice about each gift as it is opened and act grateful, even if it is a toy or book he dislikes or already owns.

Send thank-you notes: Although thank-you notes have fallen by the wayside with some time-pressed families, it's important to teach your child that thank-you notes are always the rule after birthdays and holidays.

Favors & Prizes

AT MOST BIRTHDAY and holiday parties, favors are a must. These sweet surprises are a gift from the hosting family to friends, and they should be fun to receive and to give. In many of our parties, we list favor ideas for you to pick and choose from. Use the list — and the following pointers — and your prizes will shine.

Give all guests the same favors: It's easiest if everyone gets the same party favors, including the host child. Buy favors in bulk at party stores or from catalogs, such as the Oriental Trading Company (see page 214). Or, purchase sets that can be divided up among the guests, such as a child's tea set for a tea party.

Opt for cleverness over priciness: In choosing favors, it's better to use your wits than your money. Offer some wonderful surprise that has to do with the theme, such as a gold medal for a sports party or a whistle at a police party.

Stick to reliable standbys: You can't go wrong with the classic party favors, such as penny candy, yo-yos, coloring books, magnets, markers, bubbles, plastic animals, and jump ropes.

Craft favors: Favors don't need to be store-bought. Have your child make baked goods, a computer-generated coloring book, or play clay. Send party crafts home as favors, too.

Leave room for prizes: Party favors don't all have to come packaged in a bag. They can be received as prizes, collected from a treasure chest, or scooped up under a piñata.

Party Bags

Sure, store-bought party bags are quick and easy, but they're expensive, too. Here are some clever homemade versions.

◆ **Balloon Bags:** For older kids, tuck an assortment of favors into a balloon, then blow it up.

◆ **Colorful Bags:** Purchase colored paper bags at a craft store, then personalize them with stickers or stamps.

◆ **For other creative favor bags, see the Take-Home Tackle Box on page 63 and the Bunny Bag on page 185.**

Mermaid Party, page 42

Chapter Two

Birthday Bashes

Barnyard ★ Disco Dance Club ★ Jungle ★ Firefighter ★ Flower
Cowboy Hoedown ★ Mermaid ★ Butterfly ★ Backwards ★ Puppy
Spy ★ Ladybug ★ Clown School ★ Fishing ★ Cinderella
Miniature ★ Construction ★ Painting ★ Pirate

FOR MANY parents, planning a birthday party is an annual tug-of-war between our idealism and our pragmatism. We want our child's birthday to be a blast — a person turns six only once, after all — but we don't want to have to break the bank or take a week off from work to do it.

In hopes of finding a happy middle ground, we at *FamilyFun* magazine have put together this birthday party chapter with 50 pages of ideas for throwing parties that won't throw you.

First, with the help of experienced party parents (and their willing kids), we cooked up themes with kid appeal, from a puppy party for frisky preschoolers to a spy party for that ever mysterious group, preteens. In choosing invitations, favors, games, and food, we focused on ideas that are high in fun but low in work and cost.

Also in this chapter, we feature fabulous birthday cakes that will garner *ooh*s and *aah*s, but that won't take all day to bake and decorate. And should you want your partyers to burn off energy bashing a piñata, check out our hot-air balloon (page 17).

So, go ahead and tear the wrapping off this birthday package, beginning with the tips below. We think it's a gift that should delight both party planners and partygoers alike.

Start planning early: About six weeks before your child's birthday, start planning his or her party. Together, flip through this chapter and pick a theme

Birthday Bashes

Birthday Party Checklist

Before guests arrive, make sure you're ready to party with this handy checklist:

✓ Supplies for crafts, games, and activities
✓ Prizes
✓ Favor bags
✓ Cake and ice cream
✓ Birthday candles
✓ Camera (and extra film)
✓ First aid kit
✓ Party clothes

that suits his or her current passion, whether it's princesses or pirates.

Don't break the bank: Once you've settled on a theme, adapt the party so it works within your budget. To cut costs, use just one or two of our favor or craft ideas; if this is the year you want to go all out (remember, you'll have to top it next year), take our ideas and run with them.

Customize the party plan: If your four-year-old would rather be a purring cat than a puppy, you'll find these themes (and any others in this book, for that matter) easy to modify. Get creative and mix and match any of our games, foods, or favors.

Involve the birthday child: Preparing for a party can be as entertaining as the event itself. In the week prior to the party, give the birthday child a task to complete each day, such as crafting a decoration or assembling favor bags. Not only will they make fun after-school activities, but they'll also harness a child's excitement for the big day.

Be flexible hosts: No matter how much planning you do, birthday parties take on a life of their own. Picky eaters, sore losers, and kids revved up from too much cake are par for the birthday course. Have tricks up your sleeve — noncompetitive games, familiar foods, and extra prizes — as well as a sense of humor and a positive attitude, and the party will be the hit of your child's year. For more party planning tips, see page 9.

Puppy Party, page 50

Barnyard Bash

PRESCHOOLERS ARE IN HEAVEN when down on the farm. They revel in the sublime mix of baby animals, rambling tractors, and big piles of hay. If you've got a barnyard aficionado in your brood, throw this old-fashioned hoedown, which plays to their love of make-believe.

Invitations

Barnyard Invitation

THROW OPEN the barn doors on this clever invitation to see what all the racket's about. A squealing pig is inviting all the neighborhood kids to a farm party. To make one, start by cutting out a barn shape from red card stock. Cut and fold back a set of barn doors and loft doors. Next coat the perimeter of the barn's back (avoiding the doors) with a glue stick and press firmly onto white card stock. Carefully cut around the barn, then outline the roof. Write down the party details on the inside and put a pig sticker in the loft to spread the word.

barn's rounded roof). Fold the smaller side flaps in toward the middle to work as supports. Next cut out barn doors with an X-Acto knife (parents only). Decorate the barn with red tempera paint and add trim with white tape. Now raise the roof by taping together a few sheets of white poster board (end to end), lightly creasing them to round

Down on the Farm Decor

HOST THIS PARTY outdoors so you won't be picking hay out of the rug for the next year. Spread a red-checked tablecloth on a picnic table and scatter the area with hay. Build a big red barn out of a large rectangular box like the one pictured on page 26. To make the barn, use scissors to round the front and back flaps on the top of the box (this will form the

Animal Dress-Up

Barnyard Bash

Farm Fun

simple. A yellow feathery headband and a plastic beak suggests a chicken, and a set of pink ears and plastic snout screams pig.

As each animal is ready, let him or her play in the pretend barn. Horses can practice jumping, cows can be milked, donkeys can no doubt be stubborn. Encourage each animal to practice her sound, waddle, or walk. Because this kind of play can escalate into horsing around, plan some quiet activities, too. The kids might choose their animal names or pretend to take a nap in a pile of hay. This will keep the play tame and fun for even the shyest goose.

Farm Fun

AFTER THE ANIMALS have had their fill of fun in the pretend barn, play classic farm games that everyone knows the rules to, such as pin the tail on the donkey, the farmer in the dell, or duck, duck, goose. Make sure everybody wins in the end.

Lost Animal Search: It's the farmer's job to call all the animals in from the pasture, but sometimes an animal gets lost. To play this game, the kids, now pretending to be farmers, must find all the lost animals (a slew of plastic or stuffed animals that have been hidden in the yard) and bring them back safely to the barn before sundown.

Prizes in a Haystack: For this game, you'll need inexpensive candy and prizes — and a big pile of hay. Hide the treats in the hay, then give each child 2 minutes to dig through and find a handful to take home.

Wagon Hayride: You could, of course, set up a real hayride for the children, if you know of a farm or stable that provides such a ser-

Barn Dance

FamilyFun reader Vicki Haugen of Hawley, Minnesota, took a cue from her son's favorite book, *Barn Dance!* by John Archambault and Bill Martin, Jr., and threw a barn party. They converted their garage into a barn with straw bales, feed sacks, horse tack, and cornstalks. Two old-time musicians brought the "barn" to life, luring guests dressed in western attire to kick up their heels.

the roof, and taping them atop the barn. It should take you less than an hour to set up the barn — the preschoolers' imaginations will fill in all the missing details.

Animal Dress-Up

AS KIDS COME to the door, grown-up farmers (parents dressed in overalls) can turn them into their favorite animals. Along with face paints or store-bought animal noses, have construction paper on hand to make headbands with ears. Be prepared to design most anything: horses, cows, donkeys, sheep, goats, pigs, dogs, cats, chickens, roosters, ducks, and geese. Remember to keep the ideas

Animal Sounds Bingo

vice. In lieu of real horses and hay wagons, it's almost as thrilling to young kids to be pulled around the yard in a little red wagon filled with hay.

Animal Sounds Bingo: To make each game card for this farm version of bingo, draw a grid on a square of paper. Add a star in the center square for a free space and fill each remaining square with a sticker from a set of eight different animals (making sure each card has a mixture of the same animals). To play, kids mark their cards with buttons when they hear a parent call out an animal noise that corresponds with a sticker. When one player covers an entire row or column on his card, he calls out "Bingo!"

Old McDonald's Farm Food

LET THE "ANIMALS" pig out on farm feed — a variety of foods that look like hay, grains, vegetables, or (to be not so delicate) slop. French fries and pasta may pass for hay; granola makes excellent grains. For dessert, pile on the pig cake.

Wagon Hayride

This Little Piggy Cake

This Little Piggy Cake

    2 baked 9-inch round cakes
    6 cups pink frosting
 1½ pink Snowballs
    2 pink Necco wafers
    2 green M&M's
    2 brown M&M's
    1 red sour gummy string

Layer the cakes and frost them pink. For eyes, place green M&M's on Necco wafers, using frosting as glue. Use one Snowball topped with brown M&M's for the snout. For ears, cut the half Snowball in half again and frost the cut edges pink. Tie the gummy sour into a Q for the tail. Serves 8 to 10.

Thank-You Notes

A POLAROID PICTURE of each dressed-up farm animal will serve as the perfect thanks. The birthday child should be in the picture, too, with his hoof around his pal's shoulders.

Favors

Let farm guests pick prize apples from a tree. To make an "apple," fill a red bandanna or fabric piece with plastic farm animals, tiny toy tractors or trucks, or farm stickers. Tie the bandannas with yarn to resemble apples and hang them from a tree for guests to pick after eating cake.

Disco Dance Club

PRETEENS LOVE TO DANCE, preferably at home alone in front of the mirror. But invite a group of them to a disco-themed birthday dance, dressed in funky '70s clothes, and they'll strut their stuff in public (even in view of the opposite sex). So crank disco CDs and watch the dance fever sweep the floor.

Retro Invites

SINCE NO PRETEEN GUY wants to be the token male at a dance party, cohost the bash with another family so you can pack your

Retro Invite

Disco Dance Club with plenty of boys and girls, plus split the costs and the planning. To make the invitation, cut bell-bottoms out of an old pair of jeans. Glue them onto folded cards, decorate with glitter glue, and write down all the party particulars, including a request to wear '70s gear (bell-bottoms, platforms, and leisure suits).

Disco Decor

CREATE A Disco Dance Club by hanging silver and gold ceiling-to-floor streamers in your garage or family room. Rent a mirrored disco dance ball from a party supply place or make your own out of a beach ball covered with reflective stickers. Have a costume box on hand with '70s garb for the kids who thought they were too cool to dress up but wish they had when they see how much fun everyone else is having.

Fun & Games

Disco Ball Backdrop: Set up a painted backdrop to take everyone's

Dance, Dance, Dance

picture with a Polaroid camera before they step onto the dance floor. To make one, paint a large piece of Fome-Cor and glue on stars and a disco ball, both cut from aluminum foil. Paint on hip dancers and cut out face holes for posing guests.

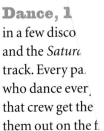

Disco B

Dance, 1

in a few disco
and the *Satur*
track. Every pa
who dance ever
that crew get the
them out on the f   .C.A.,"
the bump, or the h   _e. Pretty soon
even the most diehard dance-a-phobes
will be out there shaking some booty.
Twister: Keep the '70s theme going off the dance floor with a game of Twister (the more kids the wackier).
Leisure Suit Relay: Even the coolest preteens still like to get goofy, so take a break from the dancing and step out in the yard for a Leisure Suit Relay using the box of '70s clothes you've collected. Divide the group into two coed teams and give each one a complete outfit. Each team member has to put the outfit over his or her own clothes, then run 25 yards or so and transfer the outfit to the next kid in line. The team that dresses and undresses everyone first wins.

'70s Eats

S ET UP A MINI BUFFET beside the dance floor for grazing dancers. Since many middle schoolers actually think about the foods they eat, put out healthy stuff like carrots, celery, cheese sticks, grapes, and pita pockets that can be stuffed with cold cuts. Pack a cooler with sodas, fruit drinks, and bottled water.

Smiley Face Cake

2 baked 8- or 9-inch cakes
5 to 6 cups yellow frosting
2 mint patties
lack shoestring licorice

d frost the cakes. Make the
out of two mint patties and
add a big licorice smile.

ank-You Notes

A T CLUB CLOSING time (just before the parents arrive), take a group photo. Order multiple copies and write thank-you messages on the back.

Party Favors

Set up an area for kids to craft their own party favors. Buy cheap magnetic photo frames, glue, glitter, tiny fake gems, and stickers and set the kids up to decorate frames for the Disco Ball Backdrop Polaroids. The magnets on the back will allow them to hang the pictures in their school lockers. While they're in craft mode, let them decorate pet rocks with fur and googly eyes to take home, too.

Smiley Face Cake

29

Jungle Party

SK ANY PRESCHOOLER what he or she would like to be, and the answer is bound to be something four-legged, hairy, and hopelessly noisy — which is precisely why jungle parties are such a roaring success. In this party, kids get to pretend they're wild animals by dressing in animal headbands, hunting for peanuts, and parading around the house. Tarzan, watch out.

PARTY STATS

Ages: 3 to 5
Size: 4 to 8 kids
Length: 2 hours
Prep time: 2 to 3 hours
Cost: $5 to $8 per child

Elephant Invitations

END OUT the call to your child's favorite party animals with an unfolding pachyderm. From an 8½-by 11-inch sheet of gray paper, cut out the shape of an elephant's head and trunk and draw in the eyes and tusks. Fill in the party information, including a request that each child bring a

Elephant Invitation

favorite stuffed animal. Fold up the trunk accordion style, then fold in each ear and place in an envelope.

Jungle Decorations

URN YOUR house into a deep, not-so-dark jungle with balloons, streamers, or strings of lights in tropical colors. Cordon off an area of the party room with string and hang a sign labeled "Jungle Petting Zoo." When guests arrive with stuffed animals in tow, they can set them in a comfortingly nearby spot.

Party Animal Costumes

S ANY four-year-old will tell you, it's the stripes that make the zebra. With quick-to-make headbands, kids can decorate and don their animal alter egos as soon as they

Party Animal Costume

Catch the Lion by the Tail

Stuffed Animal Safari

If your kids have a whole zoo's worth of stuffed animals, let them host a safari, like *FamilyFun* reader Linda Schrupp of Auburn Hills, Michigan, did for her kids, Kimberly and Matthew.

First Mom hid the animals. Then the kids made paper safari hats and cardboard tube binoculars. They wore safari belts with walkie-talkies and canteens of jungle juice and set up camp — a small tent and two laundry basket cages. The "hunters" used flashlights to spot the animals, then they brought them back to "camp" and put them in the "cage." When all the animals were caught, the kids sat around camp. The animals were then free to go back to their natural habitat.

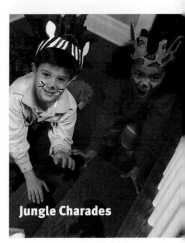

Jungle Charades

hit the party. Before the event, cut out one poster board strip (roughly 3 by 20 inches) for each guest, adding the ears for a particular animal (rounded ears for a tiger, say, or ears and horns for a giraffe). At party time, set out the strips on a newspaper-covered table or bench and scatter around a pile of crayons or water-soluble markers. Children can pick whichever blank headband they like, then color it. Measure the band around the child's head, then staple the ends so that it fits snugly. A touch of face paint — for whiskers, stripes, spots, or a black nose — completes each child's costume.

Wild Games

Jungle Charades: A great mixer for new arrivals, this game gets even the bashful hissing and howling. Before the party, cut out pictures of animals from magazines and paste them on index cards. At the party, each child gets a turn to pick a card. She must then act out her creature (no words are allowed, but animal noises are encouraged) until the others shout out her identity. When the animal is guessed, the rest of the party-goers get to jump up and act out the same animal together.

Jungle Party

Catch the Lion by the Tail: Like most winning games, this twist on duck, duck, goose combines suspense, action, and make-believe. Kids sit in a circle on the floor. One partygoer, the lion, tucks a tail (a yellow piece of fabric with a knot in one end) into his waistband and begins circling, touching each child on the head and saying "Lion." Then he touches one player on the head and shouts "Hyena!" The lion then must dash around the circle and take the hyena's spot before the hyena can grab the lion's tail. If his tail is not snatched, he remains the lion; if it is, the crafty hyena becomes the new king of the jungle.

The Great Peanut Hunt: Before the guests arrive, hide unshelled peanuts around the yard or house. At the party, explain to the kids that they, as elephants, must go out in search of a tasty meal. Give each child a plastic sand pail, then send them out to forage. Offer a prize for the partygoer who harvests the biggest crop.

Jungle Parade: A fine finale, this activity lets little ones cap off the party with a wild forest chorus. Before the party, the host parent sets up a "pawprint" trail throughout the house (poster board cutouts taped to the floor). Come parade time, partygoers gather their stuffed animals and line up behind the birthday child at the beginning of the pawprint trail. When the host parent puts on music (*The Jungle Book* sound track, for example), the kids and their pets begin their march through the jungle, continuing until the music ends.

Tiger Cake

Safari Lunch

AT ANY PARTY for preschoolers, it's smart to stick to a simple and familiar menu. Serve up peanut butter and banana sandwiches, animal crackers, jungle juice (fruit punch), and end with a roar — the tiger cake.

Tiger Cake

    1 9-inch baked round cake
    2 baked cupcakes
      Orange frosting
      Tube of chocolate decorator's icing
      Decorations: green hard candies,
        peppermint patties, chocolate
        dots, black jelly beans, and
        black shoestring licorice

Arrange the cooled round cake "face" on a platter with two cupcake "ears." Frost with orange icing. Zigzag chocolate piping on the face for stripes. Add green candy eyes, assorted chocolates and jelly beans for the nose and ears, and black licorice strings for the whiskers.

Jungle Charades

Firefighter Party

CONSIDERING THE NUMBER of kids who say they're going to be firefighters when they grow up, it's a wonder the world isn't teeming with these brave rubber-coated souls. Those flashing lights, those nifty hook and ladders, those cute Dalmatians — what preschooler wouldn't make it his career of choice? As we heard from many *FamilyFun* readers, it's also a popular birthday theme. Give this party a try, and word of your creativity might just spread like, well, you know what.

The Fire Station Decoration

THE CENTERPIECE of the party *FamilyFun* reader Susan Andrews of St. Petersburg, Florida, threw for her son was a cardboard fire truck. She cut a refrigerator box into a pickup truck shape, then decorated it with signs and pie plate headlights. She gave each child a plastic firefighter's hat, and they spent the next few hours cooking up adventures in the old pumper.

Fire Engine Cake

1 baked 13- by 9- by 2-inch cake
6 cups red frosting
¾ cup gray frosting
Decorations: red M&M's, chocolate sandwich cookies, pretzel rods and sticks, yellow gumdrops, black jelly bean, white Chiclets, mini jawbreakers, black twist and shoestring licorice

Cut the cake into four pieces (A, B, C, and D). Slice B in half horizontally to create E. Stack A onto D for the engine bed, B onto C for the cab, and E onto D for the control panel. Frost the bed and cab red and the controls gray. With frosting, place an M&M in the center of each cookie to make the wheels, then press onto the engine. Add a pretzel ladder, gumdrop emergency lights, jelly bean horn, Chiclet headlights, and jawbreaker controls. Use twist licorice to make a hose and shoestring licorice to outline the windows of the cab.

Cardboard Fire Truck

Firefighter Fun

FOR VERY YOUNG kids, the cardboard truck will probably be enough, but older ones may also enjoy these games.

Rescue Challenge: When *FamilyFun* reader Christy Hammond of Wallingford, Connecticut, threw this party, her five-year-old son and his guests had to put on a fire hat, slip down a slide, and drive a toy car across the yard to the playhouse, which was erupting in yellow posterboard flames. After picking up a length of garden hose and pretending to douse the "fire," contestants ran to a rope ladder, rescued a stuffed animal clothespinned to a tree, and drove the toy car back to the start to receive a prize.

Fire Station Tour: Christy arranged to bring her crew to the nearby firehouse, where they got to tour the sleeping quarters, sit in the front seat of a real fire truck, and even help water the firefighters' garden with the fire hose.

Red-Hot Food

FOR LUNCH, serve anything that's red (such as tomato soup) or has gentle heat (salsa and chips). Then call in a Fire Engine Cake. Like all fire trucks, it'll go fast.

Fiery Favors

Plastic firefighter hats and a short length of old garden hose make a terrific take-home dress-up set. Or, you can create a goody bag, complete with a computer-generated fire chief certificate, a Matchbox fire engine, and fireball candies.

Flower Party

EVERYTHING COMES UP ROSES — and pansies and marigolds — at this party, which celebrates a year of growth right at the grassroots level. Filled with flowers and hands-on gardening, this theme will especially be a blooming success for kids with spring or summer birthdays.

PARTY STATS
Ages: 6 to 10
Size: 6 to 10 kids
Length: 2 hours
Prep time: 2 to 3 hours
Cost: $4 to $6 per guest

Invitations

WRITE THE INVITATIONS on scented stationery (or you can use a cotton ball to dab perfume on plain paper). Add a border of flowers to each card with stickers or an ink stamp. For a finishing touch, have your child dot each *i* with a tiny daisy.

edges of the stack. Next pinch the center of the pile and tightly twist one end of a long pipe cleaner around the pinched portion. Plump the blossoms by pulling up the petals a layer at a time. Then arrange the finished bouquet in a vase or basket.

Floral Decor

A BOUQUET of giant paper flowers makes a pretty centerpiece for this birthday party. To make each flower, stack several sheets of colored tissue paper and then scallop the

Flowery Fun

Paint Petal Faces: When they arrive, turn each guest into a flower child by face-painting flowers on their cheeks and bumblebees on their noses.

Rock Garden Art

With some acrylic paints and small paintbrushes, party guests can turn a pile of stones into ornamental artwork to take home and spruce up their families' window boxes, flower beds, or indoor plants.

Prior to her birthday, ask your child to help scout around in the backyard for smooth stones in various shapes and sizes. Rinse and dry them. At the party, let the guests take turns choosing ones they'd like to paint. Encourage them to spend a few minutes discussing what each stone's shape lends itself to. A wide, rounded stone, for example, might resemble a plump frog. A group of stones may inspire a brood of ducklings or a group of ladybugs. After painting their images, the kids can use a permanent black marker to outline them or to add distinguishing details.

Pot a Plant

When her granddaughter, Brittany, was five years old, *FamilyFun* reader Carol Fitzgerald, from Wayne, Pennsylvania, turned the entire summer into a celebration of flowers. Together they planted sunflower seeds indoors and then transplanted them outside when the weather was warmer.

To document how tall Brittany's flowers grew, she and Carol began photographing members of their family for comparison. Soon the plants were taller than Brittany's sister, Kristin (age three), her cousin Haley (also three), Brittany herself, then her mom, Carol, her grandfather, and her dad. Carol put together a little album for Brittany that showed the success of her gardening project and served as a year-round reminder of their summer fun.

Decorate a Flowerpot: Next let the kids turn plain terra-cotta pots into personalized planters. All it takes is a box of Cray-Pas oil pastels (available at art supply stores). Because the oils are permanent, it's a good idea for the kids to first sketch their designs on the pot with a pencil. Then they can trace over the sketches with the pastels.

Pot a Plant: Once the pots are decorated, they're ready to fill with flowering plants the kids can take home. A flat of annuals, such as impatiens, pansies, or marigolds, is perfect for this project. Help each child pot her plant and moisten the soil. Then set the potted flowers aside for safekeeping until the party ends.

Have a Watering Can Brigade: Cap off the activities with a lively relay. Divide the kids into two teams and have the members of each line up side by side. Hand the leader of each group a watering can (empty milk jugs will do in a pinch). When the race begins, the teams quickly pass their cans down the lines to the last person. She then runs to the head of her line and begins the process all over again. The game ends when one of the team leaders returns to her original position in line.

Flower Party

An Edible Garden Party

FamilyFun reader Caitlin McCoy, age ten, from Wallingford, Connecticut, had an idea for putting her family's old kiddie pool to use. She recycled it into a kid-size garden and grew all the ingredients for a special family dinner party. She planted parsley and peppers for soup and spaghetti sauce, strawberries for a sweet treat, and marigolds to keep hungry animals away.

Flower Power Lunch Party

O NCE FLOWER PARTY guests have exercised their green thumbs potting real flowers, invite them to sit down to a berry delicious lunch.

Fruit Flowers

For a fruity appetizer, the kids can plant these flowers on their plates. Start with a slice of banana or kiwi for a flower center. Arrange raspberry or strawberry petals around it, then add a shoestring licorice stem with fresh mint leaves.

Sunflower Pockets

Spread cream cheese or your kids' favorite salad dressing inside half of a small pita. Then stuff the pocket with grated carrots, raisins, and raw sunflower seeds.

Sunny Beverages

Let everyone wet their whistles on tall glasses of sunny lemonade. Or, brew some herbal tea to serve over ice in frosty mugs or hot with honey and slices of orange or lemon.

Fruit Flowers

Sunflower Cake

Sunflower Cake

    1 baked 9-inch round cake
    5 cups yellow icing
    16 Twinkies
      Mini Hershey Kisses

Place the round cake in the center of a serving dish and frost the top and sides with yellow icing. Then top with mini Hershey Kisses (or other small chocolates) to create sunflower "seeds." Start in the center and work in circles to the outer edge. For petals, frost the Twinkies individually and place them along the outer edge of the cake, as shown. Serves 8 to 10.

Flower Favors

FILL TINY FLOWERPOTS with seed packets (choose varieties that are especially easy to grow), flower stickers, or gummy worms. Or present each guest with a small sachet of floral potpourri. Guests can also take home their potted flowers and rock garden art.

Cowboy Hoedown

R UMOR HAS IT that in Texas a man is measured by the size of his hat, the strength of his herd, and the success of his birthday bash. Reader Carrie Melson of Austin, who put together this party for her friend's son, Brandon, clearly knows how to rope 'em in.

PARTY STATS

Ages: 3 to 5
Size: 4 to 10 kids
Length: 2 hours
Prep time: 2 to 3 hours
Cost: $4 to $6 per child

Wanted Poster Invitations

N O SELF-RESPECTING cowpoke is gonna come within a mile of your ranch without a reason, so send out pictures of the birthday child on Wanted posters to round up guests.

Cowpoke Fun

Dude 'Em Up: Ask guests to wear cowboy hats to the hoedown. As they arrive, present each poke with a bandanna and a grocery bag vest. To make one, cut up the center front of the bag, then round out the neckhole and cut circles for armholes. Kids can tear a fringe on the bottom and glue on a foil sheriff's badge.

Sidewinder Jump: In this game, kids have to avoid the "bite" of a deadly rattler — an 8-foot rope. At one end, glue a piece of cardboard cut and painted to resemble a rattlesnake's head. On the

Sidewinder Jump

Dude 'Em Up

other end, create a rattle using four to six film canisters. Punch a hole in the top of each canister, then slip one canister on each end of a pipe cleaner (ball up the ends beneath the caps to keep it from slipping out). Fill each canister with dried beans or rice and glue or tape them shut. Tightly twist the pipe cleaners around the ends of the rope. To play, have kids hold the rattlesnake rope just above the rattles and whisk the rope back and forth along the ground. Children try to jump over the wriggling and rattling snake without touching it. For older kids, raise the rope a few inches off the ground.

Lasso Practice: Using a hula hoop and a child's wooden rocking horse, have cowboys try to "rope" the mustang's neck.

Shoot-out at the Better-than-OK Corral: Spread small, inexpensive plastic bugs on the sidewalk and have kids shoot at the varmints with squirt guns. Anyone who moves a bug with the stream of water gets to keep it.

Chow Wagon

SERVE UP pie tins filled with sloppy joes and glasses of sarsaparilla — root beer — to wash down the trail dust. End with cake shaped like a cowboy's best friend: his horse.

Horse Cake

  1 baked 13- by 9- by 2- inch cake
  3 cups chocolate frosting
  1 cup white frosting
  Decorations: black shoestring licorice, Life Savers candies, Necco wafer, mini jawbreaker, black jelly bean, marzipan carrots

Cut and arrange the baked cake as shown below. Frost the cake brown, adding a white frosting mane. Braid the licorice for the bridle and reins and connect them with Life Savers candies. Coil black licorice for the eye and top it with a Necco wafer and a mini jawbreaker. Give the horse a jelly bean nose to sniff his marzipan carrot treat.

Favors

FILL GOLD RUSH sacks (brown paper bags) with toy ponies, squirt guns, gummy snakes, chocolate coins, or toy harmonicas.

Horse Cake

Mermaid Party

T HROW YOUR birthday child this underwater fantasy party, and she'll dive right in. Add six to 12 mermaid-crazed friends, hidden treasure, and a slew of games and races, and she may never want to come up for air. When we ran this party in *FamilyFun* magazine, the real showstopper was the Mermaid Cake (see page 44).

Deep-Sea Invites

Deep-Sea Invite

L URE PARTY GUESTS with an underwater message. Write the details on a 5- by 6-inch piece of green construction paper with a wavy top edge. Slip it into a ziplock sandwich bag. Sprinkle sand, glitter, and confetti (available at party stores) inside. Fold in half and mail in a blue envelope.

Crown Crafting

42

Crown Crafting

Decorations

T HIS PARTY has plenty of decorations — you essentially turn one room into an ocean — but they're basic and inexpensive. First, drape a sheet over a chair to make a mermaid rock. Then hang a long green streamer, clothesline style, across part of the ceiling, attaching the ends securely with tape and thumbtacks. Cut a half-dozen fish and starfish shapes out of poster board and tape each to ends of 4-foot lengths of blue crepe paper. Hang these, plus some plain streamers, from the suspended green streamer. Litter the floor underneath with blue balloons.

Crown Crafting

T HIS QUIET icebreaker gives arriving guests a chance to settle in. Ahead of time, cut out 5-inch-high poster board crowns. On a table, set out saucers of glitter, confetti, or stickers, along with glue sticks and water-based markers or crayons. Ask partygoers to decorate their crowns. Size each by wrapping it around the child's head and stapling the ends together. Then, set the creations aside to dry for the Mer-race (see page 45).

Mermaid Games

Trail of Treasure: Nothing piques grade-schoolers' curiosity like a treasure hunt. This one relies on pictures instead of words, so the game moves quickly. To make the treasure chest, cover the outside and inside of a small Styrofoam cooler with aluminum foil. Glue two strips of black construction paper, as shown, to simulate straps. Fill with a mixture of uncooked pasta shells (large or jumbo stuffing-size works best), cooked spinach linguine "seaweed" (the gross-out factor is priceless), costume jewelry,

Trail of Treasure

Mermaid Party

Mermaid Cake

The Kimmel family of Montebello, New York, sent the blueprint for this outstanding Mermaid Cake to *FamilyFun* magazine. The cake is large enough to feed a big group of kids and still have leftovers.

1 baked 8-inch round cake
1 baked 13- by 9- by 2-inch cake
12 baked cupcakes
8 cups frosting (white, blue, and yellow)
Necco wafers (pink, green, and purple)
2 green Necco wafers and 2 blue M&M's
    for eyes
Shoestring licorice eyelashes
Fruit by the Foot mouth
Colored sugar

Cut and arrange the cakes as shown above. Frost the mermaid's tail blue and cover it with Necco wafers. Frost the head and body white (or whatever skin color you choose) and the bikini top blue. Add the candy eyes and mouth. Frost the cupcakes yellow, then sprinkle on colored sugar for a marine sheen.

Sea Food

Anything ocean related, and preferably punny, makes a great catch of the day for this party — peanut butter and jellyfish, potato boats, or shell pasta sprinkled with "sand" (grated Parmesan). Serve with blue Gatorade and Goldfish crackers. For dessert? A bowl of blue Jell-O and gummy fish or the Mermaid Cake above.

plastic ocean creatures, or chocolate coins.

To set up the hunt, collect eight beach items — a swim mask, a shell, a flip-flop, and so on. On small pieces of paper, draw a picture showing the location of each item and of the treasure chest. (Hide the chest in a spot where all the kids will be able to gather easily.) Place the picture of the chest inside, say, the shell and hide that. Tape the picture of the shell inside the flip-flop, and so on, until you've hidden all but one clue. Give the remaining picture to the kids and instruct them to follow the clues in order. When the

chest is found, each child gets a turn reaching into it and fishing for one or two treasures.

Skin the Eel: Kids have to work together to complete this flexibility challenge. First line up everyone single file. Each child bends forward and places his right hand back through his legs and with his left hand grasps the right hand of the player in front of him. The player at the back of the line lies down on his back while everyone else walks backward over him. The next player lies down, then the next, until everyone is on their back. The last player to lie down gets up and walks forward, pulling the rest of the line with her, until all are standing and still holding hands.

Mer-race: This game made a big splash with our kid-testers, who stayed all wrapped up for the rest of the party. First outfit each child with a mermaid tail by having him or her step into a heavy-duty drawstring trash bag. Tie the bag loosely around the child's waist, then secure it in place with a belt of duct tape. Wrap a second strip of duct tape around the knees to create a fin effect, then lay the children down on their bellies across the room from your mermaid rock. Scatter the crowns around on the rock. At the "Ready, set, dive" signal, kids squirm and flap their way to the rock, don their crowns, and race back. Afterward, photograph each child, then serve lunch. (Cut a few small airholes in the bags, so the kids don't end up with slimy fish feet.)

Thank-You Notes

KIDS ALWAYS love seeing pictures of themselves in costume. To make a thank-you card, fold a piece of construction paper in half, cut four angled slits on front, and slip in a photo of each child as a mermaid. Add a silly message like "Nice to sea you" or "Come back off fin!"

Favors & Goody Bags

After a day at the beach, send kids home with a plastic or tin pail full of treasure — squirty fish, ocean stickers, fish pencils, real shells, and chocolate coins. Top it off with a sprinkling of sand or glitter.

Skin the Eel

Butterfly Party

PARTY STATS

Ages: 3 to 5
Size: 4 to 8 kids
Length: 2 hours
Prep time: 2 to 3 hours
Cost: $4 to $6 per child

WE KNOW A KID who called butterflies "flutter-byes," a little linguistic mix-up that, to our minds, makes a lot of sense. But whatever your child calls them, we think she'll find that throwing a butterfly birthday party is a sure way to attract friends. Invite a brood of caterpillar-loving kids over for the afternoon and watch them metamorphose into butterflies with fluttering wings.

Take Wing

When guests arrive, transform them into butterflies — and their imaginations will soar. To make a set of wings, draw wings on cardboard or poster board, measuring from the child's hips to her head with a wingspan that reaches no more than 8 inches beyond her shoulders. Cut the wings out with a utility knife. Punch four holes and thread with ribbon to create two straps.

Lastly, allow the kids to add personal touches with markers, colored cellophane, and glitter glue. To don the wings, the child should slip one arm through each strap and wear the wings like a backpack.

Fluttery Decor

TURN YOUR HOUSE into a Monarch's Palace by decorating the party room with watercolor butterflies. To make one, dab watercolors in patterns on a coffee filter. Once dry, pinch the filter in the middle like a bow tie and slide a clothespin in place. Fan out the wings, add construction paper antennae, and clip to curtains, tablecloths, and even the telephone cord. This also makes an engaging party craft (and take-home favor).

Butterfly Wings

the butterfly that can escape from the cocoon without help. Switch places.

Butterfly Relay: Break into two lines. Place a bunch of toy butterflies 20 feet from a starting line. Hand the first two players nets. The object is for each child to catch a butterfly, run back, and pass the net to the next. The team who catches the most wins.

Butterfly Grilled Cheese Sandwich

High-Flying Fun

Hunt for Nectar: Before the party, hide foil-wrapped flower candies around the yard. At the party, offer guests paper bags and tell them it's their job as butterflies to find the nectar: the flowers.

Cocoon Wrap: Partner up the kids and give each pair a roll of toilet paper. Have one child hold the roll's loose end while the other holds the roll. At "Go!" let the cocooning commence. See who reaches the end first, then find

Butterfly Lunch

Serve up Butterfly Grilled Cheese Sandwiches, peach nectar, and fruit salad. To make a sandwich, cut wings from a grilled cheese, add a celery stick body, cherry tomato and carrot stick antennae, and veggie spots. Instead of cake, try Gelatin Butterflies (below).

Favors & Prizes

Fill nets with toy butterflies, flower seeds, gummy caterpillars, or candies.

Fluttery Creations

Butterfly fans will flutter at the sight of sweet Gelatin Butterflies. In a medium-size bowl, dissolve 6 ounces of blue gelatin dessert with 1 cup of boiling water. Pour the mixture into an 8-inch square pan and refrigerate for at least 3 hours. Using a 2½-inch butterfly cookie cutter, carefully cut out the gelatin. Alternatively, make a butterfly stencil on waxed paper, place it on the gelatin, and cut around it with a knife. If the butterflies are difficult to remove, dip the pan's bottom in warm water for a few seconds. Help your children arrange a short length of twisted licorice in the center of the wings. For antennae, insert shoestring licorice into the heads. For added color, remove several candy dots from their paper and press them into the wings.

Backwards Party

T HIS YEAR, surprise your birthday child with a wacky bash where everything is topsy-turvy, from the invitations (which must be read in a mirror) to the cake (upside-down cupcakes). The basic party plan is to do everything from nuts to soup backwards. When guests arrive, greet them with "Bye" instead of "Hi," then follow this party plan from end to beginning.

Wacky Invitations

S ET THE MOOD for this crazy party by sending store-bought thank-you notes (get it?), or write the invitations backward on a piece of paper to be read in a mirror. Include the party dress code: clothes (and ponytails, ties, and shoes) must be worn backward.

Upside-Down Decorations

H ANG BALLOONS upside down from ribbons on the ceiling, lay streamers festively on the floor, post signs everywhere with backwards sayings (!emocleW and !yadhtriB yppaH). Set the table with chairs facing out and plates and silverware on a tablecloth on the floor under the table.

Upside-Down Decorations

Head Shots

For party entertainment, let guests pose for this trick photo that doubles as a favor. Have each guest lie on her back with a pillow propped under her head. (Her chin should be pointing up.) Apply a coat of flesh-tone face paint to conceal her eyebrows. Then, using darker shades, paint fake eyebrows on her cheeks (below her eyes) and a mouth and nostrils centered on her forehead. Top it off by tying a bandanna bandit style over her mouth and chin. Smile (er, frown) and take a Polaroid. Send it home or enclose it in a thank-you note.

Backwards Fun

KEEP THE GAMES simple at this party — it will be game enough for guests to walk around with their pants on backwards. In addition to running backwards through an obstacle course and playing pin the donkey on the tail, try these party hits.

Hint, Hint: Greet guests by saying "Good-bye!" and the guests will spend the rest of the party saying things backwards, which sometimes means you won't know if they really want a second piece of cake, or if "yes" really means "no."

Silent Chairs: Follow the rules of musical chairs, except the sitting starts when the music starts.

Inside-Out Piñata: The Trifone family of Norwalk, Connecticut, made an inside-out piñata — a big, partially inflated balloon with candy stuck on the outside — for the partyers to pop with a stick.

Sardines (aka Seek and Hide): One person hides, and the rest look for him. As they find him, each player squeezes into the hiding place until the spot is jammed with kids. When the last person finds the hiding place, that kid starts a new game by hiding first.

Gift Opening

THE YAUNS of Liberty, New York, threw a backwards birthday party where gifts were opened before the cards. The presents were incredible — clothes wrapped inside out, cards outside the envelopes, thank-you cards instead of birthday cards, and paper, ribbons, cards, and bows inside the boxes.

Far-Out Food

FOR THE MAIN course, serve birthday meatloaf cake. Bake your favorite meatloaf recipe in a round cake pan, "frost" it with mashed potatoes, and top if off with birthday candles. For a sweet ending, turn cupcakes upside down, frost them, and put a relighting candle in each, then sing "You to Birthday Happy."

Slumberless Party

Here's a backwards idea for a slumber party sent in by *FamilyFun* reader Ann C. Petersen of Southern Pines, North Carolina. Guests at her daughter's party arrived in pj's at 3 P.M. The party lasted until 10 P.M. with all the slumber party traditions, but ended before it was time to hit the sack, which meant no homesick kids at midnight.

Puppy Party

OR KIDS WHO ARE dogmatically canine, this party gives them license to bark, roll over, and gnaw on bones. From start to finish, it's got a message that will thrill them: hey, little lads and lassies, today you aren't just pretending to be a pack of Rovers — you *are* the dogs.

Puppy Party Invitations

Call In the Dogs

NVITE THE party animals to join in the fun with this invitation. Cut two matching paper squares and tape them together along the top edge. From the top one, cut away the center part and round the ears. Decorate the bottom one with a face and collar, then clip on a detachable dog tag cut from the bottom of an aluminum pie plate (bend back the tag's sharp edges). Write the child's name backwards on the tag's reverse side (so the type is embossed). Put the party info under the earflaps and ask guests to come with license in paw.

Doggy Decor

O SET UP this party, you don't need to work like a dog. Decorate the front door with a discreet "Kennel Club" sign. Inside, set up a table as the groomer's salon, with a sign to that effect and a mirror. Fill the playroom with doghouses made from large cardboard boxes — one for each kid with his name over a simple cutout door (wait until the kids arrive if you think they'll choose special puppy names). Even simpler to make are doghouse facades, cut from the sides of a box and leaned against a wall. With the addition of clean dog bowls — gauche, but they'll love it — the scene is set for playtime, games, and snacks.

Welcome Wag

50

Welcome Wag

AS KIDS COME in the door, have grown-up "groomers" turn them into puppies. Use face paint and dog ears (fabric or fake fur fastened to the child's hair with hair clips). Lay out dog-collar-making baubles including beads, buttons, string, and extra dog tags. Let the pups string their own (help them center the tag). It'll be your job to make sure nobody's necklace gets turned into a choke collar. Have an instant camera handy for portraits.

Dog Games

YOU WON'T NEED any formal games for this pack of dogs. Two hours of dressing up and remaining in character is enough to keep them howling for days about the party. Still, here are two activities in case you've got a roving pack on your hands.

The Snoop: Hide about 40 cardboard bones at "dog height" and have the puppies hunt on hands and knees. Found bones get buried in a bag at the end of the game in exchange for treats.

Dog Trainer Says: Based on Simon says, this game has the kids doing dog tricks but only when the leader prefaces the command with "-Trainer says..." The trainer will need a cheat sheet to remember appropriate dog commands: Sit. Lie down. Roll over. Speak. Jump. Shake. Stay. Three-year-olds may have trouble keeping the rules straight. For them, forget the "Trainer says" part and just pretend to teach them tricks like Sit or Run around the yard, backwards. Five- year-olds might like the game better if you add silly commands like Growl, Wag your tail, and Bark your head off. All good puppies get treats for learning their tricks.

Dog Trainer Says

Doggie Bags

Send each pup home with — what else? — a doggie bag, either plain or decorated with spots. Stuff it with the child's photograph (puppy name and breed underneath with some remark like "Loves bones" or "Beautifully groomed"). Throw in a dog figurine, stickers, a ball, and a bone cookie. And of course, leave room for the collar.

Puppy Party

A party for the Dogs

If your dog is your family's best friend, throwing a birthday party for him is not all that far-fetched. Invite a few human friends and stuffed animals over (canine pals might cause chaos). Spruce up the guest of honor with a bath. And if he's tolerant, crown him with a birthday hat. And don't forget about the cake. Mold his favorite dog food into a one-serving torte, garnished with a dog biscuit "candle."

Canine Cake

Puppy Chow

BEGIN LUNCH with fruit leather "chews," then serve hot dogs or cheese or bologna sandwiches made with soft white bread and cut with a bone-shaped cookie cutter. For a side dish, make kibbles from those cheese- or peanut-butter-filled pretzels that look like dog treats (such as Combos). Garnish with sticks (pretzel rods). For extra fun, serve the entire lunch in a clean dog bowl (or just a regular bowl).

Canine Cake

    2 baked 9-inch round cakes
    2 baked cupcakes

    4 cups white frosting
       Red Fruit by the Foot
    1 green Necco wafer
       Junior Mints
       Small mint patties
       Black shoestring licorice
    2 gray Necco wafers

Frost the cake rounds and the two cupcakes. Wrap the Fruit by the Foot around the top edge of the cake to make the dog's collar. For the doggie tag, add a green Necco wafer. Place three Junior Mints on the edge of each cupcake paw, one on the top of the cake for the nose, and the rest in a random pattern all around the cake.

Fill out the spots with a few mint patties, outline the ears and jowls with the shoestring licorice, and add a fruit leather tongue. Finally, frost the M&M's to the gray Necco wafers for a pair of sweet puppy dog eyes.

Thank-You Note

SEND A MESSAGE from the birthday pup in dog language. For example, on the front, you might put a picture of your child with a cartoon dialogue balloon: "Woof-woof, arf, Batcar, grrrrr, woof-WOOF! Rrrr, Ralph." Translation inside: "That means, 'Thank you for the great Batcar for my birthday! Love, Ralph.'"

Spy Party

A THEME PARTY for preteens? The concept may seem suspect, but it holds a hidden lure: kids can hide behind personas and act sneaky. Some clues for parents: keep things loose (don't try to map out everything). And most importantly, hone your own stalking skills; while keeping an eye on things, let the kids think you've made like ink and disappeared.

Sleuthing Games

Invitations

Anything marked "Top Secret" will grab a partygoer's attention. For each special agent, cut down a manila folder to about 4 by 5 inches. On the inside, write the party details backwards (so invitees will need to use a mirror to read it). Pen the agent's name on the file tab, stamp the folder "Confidential," then slip the missive into an envelope for mailing.

Top Secret Invitation

Spy Party

Detective Decorations

LEAD GUESTS up to your front door with footprints drawn in chalk and by hanging a few fake "Police Line: Do Not Cross" banners.

Sleuthing Games

Who Am I?: Before the party, cut out pictures of celebrities. Each guest gets an identity pinned to his back, so that everyone but him can see it. Then, by asking yes or no questions, each child must figure out who he is.

Shadowing the Suspects: One at a time, usher guests into a private room, where they don a spy suit — a hat, trench coat, and a pipe. Stand each child in profile in front of a large piece of paper mounted on the wall. Shine a light on her, trace her outline, then write her name on the back. When all suspects have been traced, gather the kids in one room to guess who's who.

Clueless: For this takeoff on Mad Libs, compile a few short mystery stories. Copy or type out each tale, leaving blank several key words — such as a noun, a verb, or an exclamation. (Note above each space the type of word to be filled in.) Kids can take turns soliciting verbal entries to fill in the blanks — then reading aloud the hilarious results.

Lie Detector: While this bluffing card game won't prepare kids to be a spy, it gives them practice at keeping a poker face. The object is to get rid of all your cards — and catch a comrade in a lie along the way. Each player gets seven cards, and the rest are turned facedown in a drawing pile (you can use more than one deck, if necessary). The dealer lays a card or cards from his hand facedown on the table, declaring the value (for example, "Three sevens"). The next player has to add a card or cards of the next highest value (in this case, eights). If he or she has no such card, the choice is either to pick from the drawing pile — or to fake it. Any player can challenge by saying "Lie detector," and when the truth is told, whoever is wrong inherits the discard pile.

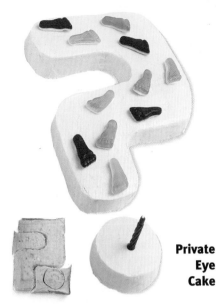

Private
Eye
Cake

Mystery Meal

WITH FOOD, anything too cute is a crime to preteens. They may prefer munchies like nachos or hot-on-the-trail mix (pretzels, raisins, and Cheez-its). For more serious eats, try pizza with the pepperoni rearranged like a question mark. As a finale, serve the Private Eye Cake.

Private Eye Cake

1 baked 13- by 9- by 2-inch cake
4 cups yellow frosting
   Gummy feet

Cut the cake as shown above. Frost with yellow icing, then walk gummy feet across the cake for footprints. For a sleuthing surprise, hide a charm in the cake before frosting it and see which spy is the sharpest (warn kids of the charm so that they eat carefully).

Thank-You Notes

BEFORE DEPARTING, each guest must ink his or her fingertips on an inkpad and leave a set of prints on an index card. Your child can use these for thank-yous later.

Shadowing the Suspects

Goody Bag

For a mysterious take-home favor, stamp "Top Secret" on the front of a manila envelope for each party guest. Inside, your gumshoes will find a pack of gum (natch), as well as top secret notepads to record evidence gathering, a pair of cheapo sunglasses, and a disguise, such as a fake nose. And don't forget the candy — even Kojak needed a lollipop to keep his observational skills sharp.

Ladybug Party

PERFECT FOR A PRESCHOOLER'S first foray into the birthday zone, this party idea will have you seeing spots — and a lot of smiles. For *FamilyFun* reader Dawne Carlson of Eagan, Minnesota, who created the party for her preschooler, Abigail, the biggest attraction was its simplicity. "At that age," she says, "a little fun goes a long way."

Fly-Away Invitations

THIS SIMPLE ladybug invitation will guarantee that your child's birthday is a lucky day. To make one, trace a 32-ounce yogurt lid onto white card stock for the ladybug's belly, and draw an outline of her head above the circle. Cut along the lines, then color the ladybug's face with markers and write the party details on her belly. Next, make the ladybug's wings by tracing the lid onto red construction paper and cutting out the circle. Decorate the circle with black spots (trace pennies for a guideline). Trim the top of the circle, cut it in half to create wings, and attach them with paper fasteners.

Fly-Away Invitations

Red and Black Decorations

ANYTHING RED and black — streamers, balloons, a tablecloth — will set the stage for this party. Dawne's guests *ooh*ed and *aah*ed over the homemade Ladybug Plates on her party table. To make one, simply decorate a red plastic plate with shoestring licorice legs and antennae (or pipe cleaners, for a non-candy version). Four chocolate cookies make up the edible spots.

Ladybug Plate and Adorable Antennae

Adorable Antennae

AT THE DOOR, greet each child with a set of his own antennae, or the materials to craft one. To make a set, twist two black pipe cleaners around a red headband. Then stick red spray-painted Styrofoam balls onto the ends of the pipe cleaners and wear.

Ladybug Games

WITH ANY LUCK, flying around the yard in ladybug antennae will keep the partyers entertained. But here are a few structured games to heighten the fun.
Stick the Spot on the Ladybug: For young kids, you'll probably want to do away with the blindfold. Just challenge them to pin a black construction paper spot onto a poster board ladybug.
Dance the Jitterbug: It doesn't matter if the guests don't know the steps; simply put on some tunes and let them make it up as they go.

Ladybug Cake

READER CAROL ZEMANEK of Shoreline, Washington, gave her four-year-old a dose of good luck with this adorable Ladybug Cake (she baked the cake in a stainless bowl).

   1 baked dome cake (made in a 1½-quart bowl or 6-inch sphere)
   1 baked cupcake
   3 cups red frosting
   12 Junior Mints

Ladybug Cake

   2 green gumdrops
   Black shoestring licorice

Turn the cake and cupcake upside down and frost them with red icing. Place the mints on the body for spots. Add the green gumdrop eyes and the licorice antennae. Serves 8 to 10.

Party Favors

GETTING TO WEAR the antennae home may be enough of a treat for this set, but you could also give each ladybug a bag with some black and red jelly beans, ladybug stickers, or Eric Carle's *The Grouchy Ladybug* (HarperCollins Juvenile Books).

Bug Party

FamilyFun reader Dana W. Fiore of Hopatcong, New Jersey, chose a Goin' Buggy theme for her son's fourth birthday party. She filled the house with yarn spiderwebs and giant balloon bugs. The kids crafted bugs with foam ball bodies, pipe cleaner legs, and googly eyes, and played Pin the Antenna on the Bug. They even made a bug piñata! The biggest hit was the treasure hunt for a picnic basket full of goodies.

Walk the Tightrope

Clown School

To COMICALLY inclined kids, life is a three-ring circus. No trick is too silly, no joke too dumb. Our clown school party is a mix of the finest circus games, events, and snacks — just the right atmosphere for a hilarious, if over the (big) top, birthday afternoon.

Balloon Invitations

WHAT BETTER herald of an arriving circus than bright balloons? To make the invitations pictured on page 7, blow up a pair of balloons for each guest and write the relevant information on the outside with permanent markers (don't knot the balloon). Deflate and place them in a bright envelope with a handful of confetti.

Circus Decorations

SPLASHED with red, blue, and yellow balloons, streamers, and tablecloths, an ordinary room or porch takes on the gaiety of a circus tent. If you have time, make posters portraying guests as three-ring circus performers. "Ladies and Gentlemen … we bring you Paul the Fire-Eating Kid!"

Clown Costumes

Clown School

Clown Costumes

AT HER DAUGHTER Jennifer's clown party, *FamilyFun* reader Lucy Hutchison of Hayes, Kansas, gave guests the option to come dressed as clowns, and they did. If your guests don't show up in clown gear, have lots of clownlike clothes and accessories — oversize shorts, shirts, jackets, gloves, suspenders, and bow ties — on hand. A parent or teen can run a face-painting table, where each child receives the necessary red nose, arched brows, pink cheeks, and exaggerated smile or frown.

Clowning Around

Heads Up: To play this catching game, each child will need a special hat you make ahead of time plus a small, soft ball, such as a beanbag or Koosh ball. To make one hat, glue two plastic bowls bottom to bottom and fashion a chin strap by either stapling on an elastic band or looping one through tiny holes. To play, put kids in pairs about 4 feet apart. At the whistle, the first player to toss the soft object into his partner's hat wins. For another variation, kids are on their own. The first child to toss the object into her own hat wins. (A photo opportunity if there ever was one.)

Walk the Tightrope: Even acts of daring are funny business when you are a clown. To set up this high-wire routine, place a 2 by 4 on the floor or ground and gather your materials: an umbrella and a large-format (but not too thick) hardcover book. In this elimination game, each contestant first crosses the high wire with an umbrella in hand. All who survive make it to round two: crossing with a book on their heads. All who live through that ordeal go to round three: crossing with the book on their heads and the umbrella in their hands. All masters of the high wire win a prize.

Balloon Sandwich: This race, a feat of cooperation, is best held outside or in a spacious room. Begin by choos-

Heads Up

Balloon Sandwich

Circus Food

ALL CLOWNS get hungry for a little circus food, so serve up hot dogs, along with a circus snack — popcorn, peanuts, or Cracker Jacks — and Ice-Cream Clown Cones.

Ice-Cream Clown Cones

This dessert proves that birthday cakes need not always take center stage. For easier handling, make the cones in batches of four. Place four scoops of ice cream on a cookie sheet lined with waxed paper, then wedge on chocolate-dipped ice-cream cone hats. Decorate each face with candy and coconut.

Freeze for at least 2 hours, then peel off and place on dessert plates. Alternatively, you can let partyers dress up their own ice-cream clowns for dessert.

How do you paint a rabbit? With Hairspray

Clown School Favor

Favors & Prizes

IN HONOR of the legendary hobo clown, favors and prizes can go in a bandanna on a stick. Load it up with gag gifts, small joke books or jokes handwritten on slips of paper (a good project for the birthday child or an older brother or sister), clown and circus animal stickers, noisemakers, candy, and funny dress-up items, such as bulbous clown noses or fake eyelashes.

Ice-Cream Clown Cone

ing partners and lining them up back to back at a starting line. Place a balloon between the partners so that they must squish it to keep it off the ground (no hands!). At the sound of a whistle, the pairs must take off in this position, shuffling their way toward a finish line. If the balloon pops or drops, they must return to the starting line for a replacement. The first sandwich to cross the line wins.

Clown Class Relay:
Here's another game for a spacious area. Ask all the kids to strip back down to their original (well-fitting) clothes and stocking feet, then divide the crew into two relay teams positioned at a starting line. At the finish line, place two similar clown outfits that include giant shorts, suspenders, a jacket, a hat, and the biggest pairs of men's shoes you can find (clomp, clomp). When the starter whistle blows, the first person from each team runs and puts on the outfit (over his clothes), runs back, strips, and tags the next player, who puts on the outfit and runs and touches the finish line, runs back, strips, and so on. The team to complete the relay first is victorious.

POPCORN "1 TICKET"

Backyard Big Top

Every year, *Family Fun* reader Mindy Malone of Naperville, Illinois, organizes a backyard circus. The stars are ten neighborhood kids. Each child chooses an act and meets at Mindy's house for rehearsals.

Their circus personalities have included a ringmaster, popcorn man, lion and lion tamer, bareback rider (on a bouncing hobbyhorse), tightrope walker (on a balance beam), strongman, tattoo man, snake charmer, acrobat (performing on a swing set and rings), and, of course, clowns. The shows are lots of fun, and everyone looks forward to the next time the circus comes to town.

Fishing Party

WE FELL HOOK, line, and sinker for this party, which *FamilyFun* reader Amy Diaz of Kingwood, Texas, threw for her five-year-old son, Christopher. The fledgling anglers in your own family are sure to be lured to this backyard fishing fest.

Go Fish Invitations

Paper Plate Fish

WRITE THE PARTY information on a cutout paper fish with a small bag of gummy worms pinned to its mouth.

Fishing Fun

GO FISH, PIN THE HOOK on the fish, and other classics work for this theme, but for Amy's crew, the most popular game was Go Goldfishing — a chance to land a real fish.

Sail High Seas: Create a fishing boat play area by spreading out a blue tablecloth and setting an overturned table on top. Drape sheets over the legs to form the hull and rig with ropes. Give kids paper towel tubes for spyglasses, a compass and map for direction, and let them sail away on a pretend boat ride. For added fun, tell tales about Sinbad the Sailor or cast for fish with magnets.

Magnet Fishing: Haul in the catch of the day by angling for paper fish with paper clip mouths. Use heavy card stock to create fish (make some temptingly bigger than others). Scatter them in an empty blue kiddie pool or painted box and hand kids poles (sturdy sticks with yarn "lines" and magnet "hooks").

Go Goldfishing: Put live goldfish in a kiddie pool of water and let the kids watch them swim around. Toward the

Magnet Fishing

Fish Cake

end of the party, each child can fish one out with a net and take it home in a ziplock bag along with fish food. (Note: Parents may not be thrilled by an unexpected pet. You can keep it a surprise for the kids, but make sure parents are comfortable with the idea when they call to R.S.V.P.)

Salty Eats

COVER YOUR TABLE with a fishing net and turn paper plates into fish by adding paper fins, tails, and heads. Serve fish and chips followed by this Fish Cake.

Fish Cake

    1 baked 13- by 9- by 2-inch cake
    2 cups orange-yellow frosting
    6 cups blue frosting
    1 peppermint patty
    1 gummy fish
      Necco wafers

Cut and arrange the cake as shown. Frost the cake blue and add yellow-orange fins and tail. Place the Necco wafers on as scales. Add the mint as an eye and the gummy fish for the mouth.

Take-Home Tackle Box

YOUNG ANGLERS will deem this grown-up-looking tackle box "reel" cool. Before the party, spray-paint Styrofoam egg cartons, then glue a cardboard handle on top. At the party, set out bowls of rubber fish, gummy worms, and tiny toys and let each child select a handful to go in his box. Send this tackle box home with the partygoer along with the bag of fish food for the goldfish.

Take-Home Tackle Box

Cinderella Party

O N SAMANTHA MILLER'S sixth birthday, a fairy tale came true. Her parents, *FamilyFun* readers Jim and Sara Miller of Aurora, Ohio, helped reenact the Cinderella tale, with each partygoer playing the belle of the ball. Samantha is older now, long past Cinderella parties, but she still keeps on her bedside table the little corked jar of fairy godmother dust from her party.

Fairy-Tale Invitations

K EEP THE invitations simple for this grand affair. Photocopy a picture of Cinderella. Ask guests to come dressed in "rags"and be prepared to get transformed into princesses.

The Party Plot

Cinderella Housecleaning

When the guests arrive, announce that each girl is now Cinderella and give each one a rag or feather duster to clean up a room in your house. (Sara reports that the guests loved this part.)

Castle Cake

Cinderella Snapshots

FamilyFun readers Mike and Sherry Branch of Fort Worth, Texas, held a ball in honor of daughter Rebecca's sixth birthday. They solved the tale's transportation problem by creating a magical "carriage" to take guests to the castle. The coach was made by mounting a cardboard facade to a wagon (you can also use Fome-Cor). The girls really enjoyed being pulled by the Duke from one room into the "ballroom" and having their pictures taken. Be sure to have doubles of the photos developed. Slipped into the thank-you notes for each girl, the pictures are wonderful reminders of being a "Princess for a Day."

The Duke Arrives

While the Cinderellas are busily dusting, the Duke (Dad dressed in a tuxedo) should knock at the door and drop off the royal invitations (in gold ink with a crown drawn on top) to the Prince's Ball.

Dressing for the Ball

The girls' excitement over the mysterious Duke will end when they realize they have nothing but rags to wear to the ball. So let them make their own gowns — simple, sandwich-board-style dresses that can be cut beforehand from extra-wide sheets of crepe paper bought from an art supply store. They can glue faux jewels, sequins, and beads on their dresses and tie a long piece of lace around their waists. Give each girl a party store tiara to keep.

Ballroom Dancing

When all the Cinderellas are dressed for the ball, play the "Nutcracker Suite" and let them dance around a living room-turned-ballroom. From time to time, turn off the music and present a prize to "the best twirler" or "the most elegant couple." (For her daughter's party, Sara had written out these awards ahead of time; everyone received a prize: a Cinderella paper doll with little rags and little gowns to wear.)

The Strike of Midnight

During the last dance, the clock strikes 12 (an alarm clock that chimes). Instruct the girls to run, leaving one shoe (slipper) behind. Back in poor Cinderella's room, they strip down to their "rags."

Find the Lost Slipper

Meanwhile, the Duke should gather up the lost slippers and fill them with party favors, such as candy and penny jewelry. Then set out a trail of aluminum foil footprints leading to the slippers. The girls should follow the footprints to their surprises.

Party Food

WHEN EACH girl has her slipper back (they fit perfectly), it's time to celebrate. At the table each girl receives a small jar of fairy godmother dust (sparkles) and a slice of Castle Cake (with ice-cream-cone towers, a graham cracker drawbridge, and candy decorations).

Wizard of Oz Party

If your kids are into playacting at parties, reenact *The Wizard of Oz* as *FamilyFun* reader Kathy Lecate of Richmond Heights, Ohio, did for her daughter's sixth birthday. The kids followed a crepe paper rainbow downstairs into Oz, where they picked a lollipop from a tree in a cardboard Munchkin Land and played Pin the Badge on the Lion. The kids were truly amazed. Imagine an entire kindergarten class skipping around a painted yellow brick road in the basement singing, "We're off to see the Wizard!"

Miniature Party

IF THERE'S ONE THING your average six- to nine-year-old would like better than a really, really big birthday bash, it would have to be a really, really small one. For this party, go ahead and scale everything down — except the guest list. The kids will marvel at the incredible shrinking details, from the tiny entryway to the world's smallest cake.

PARTY STATS

Ages: 6 to 9

Size: 6 to 10 kids

Length: 2 hours

Prep time: 2 to 3 hours

Cost: $4 to $6 per guest

Invitations

AN INVITATION that arrives in a 2-inch envelope is hard to turn down — especially if you have to read it with a magnifying glass. To make one, print the party information by hand or on a computer using letters that are at least ¼ inch tall. Then take it to a copy shop and reduce it to as small a size as you can while still keeping it legible. Stuff the mini invite into a small store-bought envelope and hand-deliver.

Decorations

CUT THIS birthday party down to size by setting up a miniature party room. For a shrunken entranceway, cover the door frame with a large piece of cardboard painted to look like the front of a small house. Then cut a door that's just big enough for the guests to crawl through. Inside the room, set up kid-size chairs, hang mini balloons, and string tiny birthday banners.

Miniature Invitation

Teeny Tiny Decorations

Fun & Games

Mini Treasure Hunt: Hide a few dozen tiny treasures around the house — dollhouse miniatures, gumball machine toys, small polished rocks, worry dolls, beads, or scaled-down candies or stickers. (Nothing in the hunt should be bigger than your thumb.) Give partygoers magnifying glasses and

66

Mini Pool

mini paper bags to collect all their treasures. Once everything is found, divvy them up so each child has an equal number to take home.

Mini Pool: Craft a mini pool table out of a shoe box and a slightly larger lid. Turn the box upside down and tape small paper cups in the four corners. Cut a 1½-inch slit across each corner of the lid, set it on top of the box, and bend the flaps into the cups. Glue on green felt. Now rack gumballs with a pipe cleaner triangle and aim with wooden pencil cues.

Tiny Bubble Blowing: Send partygoers outside to a big tub of bubble solution. Let them choose from pieces of screen, sieves, colanders, and slotted spoons to use as instruments in their final challenge: blow the world's smallest bubble.

Mini Menu

W HEN PLANNING your menu, think small. Anything mini will do, such as mini pizzas or burgers, either store-bought or homemade. Serve the meal on plastic doll or tea set plates and pour punch into

small paper cups. For dessert, serve Teeny Tiny Cake.

Teeny Tiny Cake

> 2 tablespoons fondant (available at cake decorating stores)
> Cornstarch
> 2 sandwich cookies
> 2 teaspoons frosting
> Food coloring
> Mini sugar flowers

Roll out a walnut-size piece of fondant to ¼ inch thick, dusting with cornstarch as needed. Stack the cookies and frost them together with 1 teaspoon of frosting. Frost the "cake," then drape with fondant, trimming the edges. Using a clean paintbrush, make designs with food coloring thinned with water. Decorate with sugar flowers and half a candle. Serves 1.

Party Favors

In addition to the treasures found in the mini hunt, let guests craft miniatures to take home out of emptied match, raisin, or jewelry boxes. They might make dump trucks with button wheels, tiny beds with cotton ball pillows, or wagons with pipe cleaner handles.

Teeny Tiny Cake

Construction Party

GIVEN THEIR NATURAL INCLINATION to build, it's a wonder all children don't grow up to be city planners. This outdoor party invites kids to create a pretend city booming with buildings, roads, and bridges. At noon, they break from work to enjoy a builder's lunch — complete with a dump truck full of birthday cake.

PARTY STATS

Ages: 3 to 5
Size: 4 to 6 kids
Length: 2 hours
Prep time: 2 hours
Cost: $4 to $6 per guest

Road Sign Invitations

DIRECT CONSTRUCTION workers to your site by sending out road sign invitations. To make one, cut two identical squares of yellow paper, place a Popsicle stick in between (as a signpost), and glue together. In black capital letters, write the party details on both the front and back, including a request for workers to bring

Road Sign Invitation

their favorite construction toy (forklifts, dump trucks, and front-end loaders encouraged) and to dress in work clothes.

Building Site

TRANSFORM YOUR backyard into a construction zone with yellow caution tape, orange cones, and any construction toys your child owns. If you're feeling ambitious, you might also hang homemade poster board street and traffic signs (the humor of "Children at Play" and "Go Slow: Children" signs may be lost on kids, but not on their parents). In the event of rain, clear space in your biggest room and set up the construction party there.

Fun & Games

Build a City: Near a sandbox in your backyard, set up boundaries, approximately 8 by 10 feet, for a bustling city-to-be. Before the guests arrive, set out materials and build just enough of the city to inspire the kids to take over. You might begin constructing

Build a City

Dump Truck Cake

a cardboard box building, a wood chip road, or Popsicle stick railroad tracks. For a pond, bury a bowl of water in the sandbox. Invite each arriving guest to contribute to the new city. Once the whole crew is assembled, allow enough free time for kids to complete the city.

Foreman Says: Follow the same rules as Simon says, but the child in charge should call out construction commands. He might say, "Dig with a shovel," "Use a hammer," "Mix the cement," or "Drive a truck."

Brick by Brick Relay: Party-goers race to be the first team to construct a pretend brick wall. In the weeks before the party, save empty cereal boxes, shoe boxes, and other cardboard packaging to use as "bricks." Divide the bricks into two piles and have the kids break into two teams. The first players grab a brick, race a specified distance, and lay their bricks down to begin the wall. Each child in line continues until one team completes their contract.

Bag Lunch

DELIVER sandwiches and chips to the construction site (in brown lunch bags, of course). Then let the workers dig into a plastic dump truck loaded with cake and cookie crumb "dirt."

Dump Truck Cake

> 2 baked 8- or 9-inch cakes
> 2 3-ounce packages prepared
>   chocolate pudding
> 3 to 4 cups chocolate cookie crumbs
>   Clean dump truck and shovel

Cut the cake into 3-inch chunks. Layer the cake, pudding, and crumbs in the clean dump truck and serve with the shovel. Serves 8 to 10.

Favors

FOIL-COVERED chocolate cars, tiny plastic trucks, and car stickers are all favors that can be handed out in a plastic hard hat (with a black marker, you can write the party guest's name above the brim).

Plane Party

For her son Drew's fourth birthday, *FamilyFun* reader Carol Schmidt of Mukwonago, Wisconsin, took off on a plane theme. For invitations, she made tickets, complete with boarding passes. To greet guests, a door sign read "Gate 4." Inside, decorations included empty suitcases and paper clouds. She turned the dining room table into a runway by unrolling a strip of paper down the center and drawing lines and arrows on it. A strand of white Christmas lights on each side of the runway illuminated the landing strip. Favors were plastic wings, chocolate planes on a stick, and packets of roasted peanuts.

LEGO Mania

At age nine, *FamilyFun* reader and LEGO maniac Katie Lemberg of Bernardsville, New Jersey, threw a LEGO birthday bash. For decorations, she hung streamers in bright colors and put heaps of LEGOS on the floor. The kids played pin the LEGO on the LEGO, guessed how many LEGOS were in a jar, and built the tallest tower they could in 2 minutes. The hit of the party was the cake: a sheet cake topped with eight cupcakes and frosted bright blue.

Painting Party

PARTY STATS

Ages: 9 to 12
Size: 3 to 10 kids
Length: 2 hours
Prep time:
2 to 3 hours
Cost: $5 to $8
per child

ART IS A NATURAL building block for a children's party — and it's no surprise. After all, what child wouldn't love the basic concept of messing around? Painting murals, T-shirts, and even a birthday cake will make a big impression on the visiting artists.

Invitations

SET THE STAGE by sending out painter's palette invitations. Cut poster board palettes, color with "paint" dabs, and write all the party details — plus a reminder for guests to dress in old clothes or smocks.

Artsy Fun & Games

Mural Painting: At a party for *FamilyFun* reader Jill Driscoll's son, Christopher, the guests got a kick out of creating a giant mural. Instead of using butcher paper, Jill went to her local newspaper for "end roll paper" (long rolls of paper that many newspapers give away or sell for just a few dollars) and stapled it to a large fence in her yard.

Splatter T-Shirts: For a craft that doubles as a party favor, hang white T-shirts out on a clothesline, away from unintended targets, and hand out fabric paint and brushes. Then let kids flick, splatter, and sling to their hearts' content. For a funky alternative, fill plastic water guns or spray bottles with paint that's been watered-down just enough to prevent nozzles from clogging, then aim and squirt. While they have the fabric paints out, guests may also enjoy decorating inexpensive painter's caps from a hardware store.

Pictionary: For a mess-free artistic game, play a homemade version of pictionary. Before the party, make up slips of paper that name a person, place, or thing and put them in a bowl or hat. Also gather colored markers, butcher paper, and a timer. To play, tape the butcher paper to a wall and

Mural Painting

Paintbrush Puppets

break guests into two teams. Each round, a designated drawer selects a slip and attempts to illustrate the word (no speaking!) for his team to guess before time runs out.

Paintbrush Puppets: All it takes is a few brush strokes to get one of these bristle-headed puppets ready for a birthday party show. To make one, begin by applying a base coat of acrylic paint all the way around the upper handle and metal band of a paintbrush. Add facial features, creating a different expression on each side of the brush. Once the paint dries, it's showtime!

Artistic Lunch

EVEN LUNCH can have artistic flair at your painting party. Let party guests paint bread for sandwiches and dig into slices of the Artist's Palette Cake for dessert.

Sandwich Art

Using slices of white bread as a canvas, party guests can create masterpieces that are good enough to eat. Fill several paper cups with a few tablespoons of milk, then stir in drops of food coloring to create edible paint. Using the colored milk and new paintbrushes, have the kids paint pictures and designs on the bread. Toast lightly. Now the party guests can use the slices to build their own sandwiches from a platter of fixings.

Artist's Palette Cake

>1 baked 9-inch round cake
>2 cups white icing
>   Gel frosting, assorted colors
>   Fruit leather
>1 licorice twist

Cut cake as shown and frost with white icing. Using a 1½-inch round cookie cutter, cut a thumb hole in the center of the cake. Use the cutter to lightly mark the circles on the cake, then fill with various gel frosting "paints." To make the brush, wrap the fruit leather around the base of the licorice twist and fringe the ends.

Party Favors

FILL A PAINT BUCKET with a selection of art supplies, such as a paintbrush, watercolor set, play clay, crayons, or a coloring book.

Artist's Palette Cake

Art Fair

To bring parents together and provide an outlet for their kids' creativity, *FamilyFun* reader Amy Smellie of Iowa City, Iowa, hosted a neighborhood art show last year. The kids provided the artwork, and she provided backyard gallery space and food. Pictures were clipped onto clotheslines, and a card table displayed sculptures. Every artist was given a certificate of merit. And the kids still ask, "Can we have that art thing again, please?"

Pirate Party

Treasure
Hunt Map

SINCE YOUNG KIDS have a natural inclination to pillage and plunder, pirate parties are always in fashion. *FamilyFun* readers Connie and Tony Bonaccio of Shelburne, Vermont, were hooked by the flexibility and swashbuckling fun of this theme. It made their son Ben's birthday a blast.

PARTY STATS

Ages: 6 to 8
Size: 4 to 12 kids
Length: 2 hours
Prep time: 2 to 3 hours
Cost: $4 to $6 per child

Shipwreck Invitations

ROUND UP THE pirates for the party with a message in a bottle. Along with the invitation, add a few seashells and a pinch of sand to an empty soda bottle, then hand-deliver.

Hook Hands

Swashbuckling Fun & Games

ORGANIZE YOUR party around two principles — that pirates are an energetic lot, and that they like to take home lots of booty.

Treasure Hunt: Hand the Captain (the birthday child) a map covered with decades of dust (a pinch of flour). Write a message inside about a stash of treasure hidden somewhere in your yard or house. For example: "As any pirate ought to know, this is where tomatoes grow." Each guest gets to guess the answer to a riddle, and as a pack, the guests can run to wherever the clue leads and find another one. At hunt's end, be sure to hide a suitable prize, such as a stash of candy coins or the Treasure Chest Cake.

Walk the Plank: The Bonaccios secured a board across a kiddie pool with duct tape. They set toy alligators in the pool for ambience, then each child got to walk across. Upon reaching the other side, the pirate was awarded a Hook Hand (see photo). To make one, cut a slit in the bottom of a plastic cup. Cut a hook shape out of cardboard, wrap with aluminum foil, and slip it through the slit in the cup.

Make Spyglasses: Have kids cover the end of a toilet paper tube with a square of colored cellophane and fix it in place with a rubber band.

Ticktock, Find the Croc: With a little imagination, an egg timer makes a suitable crocodile. Have pirates try to locate the hidden croc by its tick, before the bell rings.

Musical Islands: Set as many hula hoops on the floor as you have guests and play music. Pirates must walk around the hoops until you turn off the tunes, at which point they must be standing inside one of the "islands" or they're out. Every few minutes, take away a hoop, until only one seafarer remains.

Pirate Grub

K EEP THE LUNCH simple, with hot dog boats (spear a paper sail with a wooden skewer and set it in a hot dog), Goldfish crackers, and the Treasure Chest Cake.

Treasure Chest Cake

> 1 baked 13- by 9- by 2-inch cake
> 6 cups chocolate frosting
> Edible treasures, such as chocolate coins, Rolo candies, chocolate almond kisses, or Necco wafers
> Red Fruit by the Foot
> Mini jawbreakers
> Candy jewels, such as candy necklaces and rock candy

Cut two triangular wedges through the center of the cake; the two remaining pieces will form the bottom and top of the chest. Place the wedges on the bottom half of the chest, as shown, to keep the chest wedged open, then frost.

To add further support for the top of the chest, stand a few large gold coins under the lid. With the "hinged" end (right side of photo) at the back, place the top of the chest on the bottom and frost. Wrap the fruit leather straps around the chest and press mini jawbreaker "nails" into the frosting along the straps. Fill the chest and the surrounding area with edible treasures and jewels.

Take-Home Loot

Y OUR PIRATES can leave with quite a haul, such as gummy fish, temporary tattoos, chocolate coins, or candy jewelry. They can dig these treasures out of the treasure chest at the end of the hunt (just be sure everyone gets an even number of prizes).

More Treasure

For directions on how to set up the ultimate treasure hunt, see page 19.

Slumber Party, page 90

Chapter Three

Everyday Parties

Rainy Day Party ★ A Child's Tea Party
Sports Jamboree ★ Backyard Camp-Out
Slumber Party ★ Playground Party

NO ONE SAYS you have to wait for an official holiday or someone's birthday to throw a party. For instance, Sharon Lawton, a *FamilyFun* reader in Martinsville, New Jersey, came up with a novel idea for celebrating her six-year-old daughter Christine's enrollment in kindergarten. The day before school started, she hosted a Bus Stop Bagel Bash for everyone who would be at Christine's stop. Her family brought picnic blankets, bagels, and cream cheese in their little red wagon, and everyone else brought their own juice and coffee. Not only did the kids have a chance to try out their new morning routine (and play with their friends), but the parents also received helpful information from the veterans. And Sharon reported that the event was the easiest party she ever organized.

On the following pages, you'll find a half dozen themes, like the Lawton's Bagel Bash, that lend themselves to a party but don't require a lot of fanfare to pull off. You can follow the plans to a T or adapt them to a party idea of your own, such as welcoming a new kid on the block or celebrating the first day of spring. Here are a few tips to get your family on a party roll.

Seize the opportunity: Don't put off until tomorrow what you can do today — or any day. If your kids are feeling antsy on a snowy, housebound afternoon, clean out your closet for an impromptu dress-up party. If the sight of the season's first apples at your local grocery store puts you in the mood for pie, pick up a bushel of fruit and a carton of vanilla ice cream. Then invite over another family for an apple-pie-a-la-mode party.

Ice-Cream Ducklings, page 79

Everyday Parties

Dates to Celebrate

For a day-to-day listing of special days, weeks, and months, check out *Chase's Calendar of Events* (NTC/Contemporary Publishing Company). This annual directory includes historical anniversaries, astronomical phenomena, worldwide festivals, celebrity birthdays, and more.

Spin a classic game into a contest: Almost any of your kids' hobbies or favorite pastimes can become an instant party theme. If your family loves playing go fish or gin rummy, for example, organize an afternoon tournament of card games. Serve sandwiches cut into diamonds, hearts, or spades along with club soda punch.

Go with the flow: The beauty of an everyday party is that there's just one agenda: having fun. So, if tea party guests would rather watch your child's newest video, pop in the movie and start making popcorn. Or if it pours during your sports jamboree, invite the players to compete in an indoor duck-footed relay (see page 79).

Build a party around an object of fun: Challenge family members to brainstorm party activities and snacks that relate to a specific item. For a penny party, you could have a penny scavenger hunt, pitch pennies, and give out penny candy. To celebrate teddy bears, your kids could spruce up their toy cubs with paper hats and bow ties for a stuffed animal parade and help bake a batch of oatmeal "porridge" cookies.

Organize an outing: Home isn't the only place to host a party. For a special treat, offer to take your kids and a couple of their friends to play miniature golf, visit a local museum, or have manicures at the beauty salon. You can even dress up as tourists and visit all the fun sites and stops in your own town.

Start a party box: Be ready for a spur of the moment party by stocking a cardboard box with balloons, noisemakers, streamers, and decorative paper cups, plates, and napkins. Periodically, add inexpensive toys and trinkets to your stash for ready party favors.

Playground Party, page 94

Rainy Day Party

IF YOU DON'T BELIEVE that clouds have silver linings, try throwing this party on the next rainy day. It features splashy games, fun learning activities, and an irresistible snack — all guaranteed to chase away your kids' wet-weather blues. And there's virtually no advance planning required, since you're likely to have all the supplies you'll need on hand. One tip: You may want to set out a few towels near the front door for drying soggy kids.

Rainy Day Fun

Rain Painting: Here's a party activity you can get underway before the guests even take off their raincoats. Hand each child a paper plate (Chinet or other uncoated plates work best) on which he or she can sprinkle a few drops of food coloring. Then have everyone walk outdoors with their plates, holding them into the rain for about one minute. For a batik effect, let the kids use a white crayon to draw a design on the plate before adding the food coloring.

Make a Rain Gauge: If it looks like the rain won't let up anytime soon, invite the kids to predict just how much of it will fall before the party ends. Then make a rain gauge together to measure it.

Start by cutting off the top of an empty plastic soda bottle (adults only) just below the contoured portion. This serves as a funnel. Use vinyl tape to cover the cut edges on both the funnel and the open bottle. With a permanent marker, draw a line on the bottle 2 inches from the bottom and then at ½-inch increments up from there. Pour in enough water to reach the first mark. Insert the funnel into the open bottle, and the gauge is ready to collect rain.

Rain Painting

Rainy Day Party

Snow Day Party

FamilyFun reader Kim Jaworski says it's the Minnesota snowstorms that get her family down. To lift their spirits, they check into a hotel and spend the day swimming in a heated pool.

Create a Cloud in a Jar:
Everyone knows that rain falls from the sky, but it actually starts on earth in lakes and oceans and evaporates upward. Once all the kids are indoors and dried off, let them create a miniature rain cycle in a jar with this quick science trick.

Fill a metal cake pan with ice and wait a few minutes so the pan gets cold. Pour 2 inches of hot tap water (parents

Cloud in a Jar

only) into a widemouthed jar. Set the pan of ice on the jar rim and watch what happens.

The hot water will evaporate, causing vapor to fill the jar. As it nears the air at the top, the vapor will cool and condense on the jar sides and the pan bottom. Explain that clouds form in the sky when water vapor condenses on particles of dust or salt. Rain falls when water droplets in the clouds collide and combine, becoming too heavy to stay aloft. If your kids watch closely, they may see a few raindrops fall into the water in the jar.

Ice-Cream Ducklings

B Y NOW, everyone will be ready for a treat. Make a splash by scooping up a brood of these Ice-Cream Ducklings.

>French vanilla ice cream or
> lemon sherbert
>Paper cupcake liners
>Chocolate chips or raisins
>Orange gumdrops
>Dried apricots or orange fruit
> leather

For each duckling's body, place a large scoop of French vanilla ice cream

Go On a Critter Hunt
Rain has a way of bringing reclusive critters, such as earthworms, frogs, and salamanders, out of hiding. If the kids are game (and dressed for showery weather), take a walk to see how many they can tally. And don't forget to keep an eye on the sky — you may spot a rainbow.

or lemon sherbert on top of a flattened paper cupcake liner. Create a neck by topping the body with a spoonful of ice cream and using the bowl of the spoon to flatten it slightly. Place a small scoop of ice cream on the neck for a head.

Ice-Cream Ducklings

Press on chocolate chips or raisins for eyes and a flattened orange gumdrop (cut into two pieces) for a beak. Finally, cut webbed feet out of fruit leather or dried apricots.

Ducky Relay

CAP OFF THE party with a wacky team race that lets contestants put their best webbed foot forward. Before the party, you'll need to make a pair of duck feet for each team. Here's how:

Draw the outline of a duck foot (about 14 inches from heel to toe) on a large piece of cardboard and use a craft knife to cut it out (a parent's job). Make the matching foot by placing the first one face side down on the cardboard and tracing and cutting around it. Next, cut a tissue box into halves and glue them on top of the feet with the box bottom facing up. Use tempera paint to color the feet bright orange or yellow. Let the feet dry thoroughly before using them.

To race, divide the kids into two teams. On the far side of the room, set up a chair for each side. When the race starts, the first player from each team, wearing duck feet over his shoes, must make his way to his team's chair, circle it, and return to the starting point while quacking and flapping his arms. The next child in line quickly puts on the shoes and takes a turn. The first team to finish wins.

Ducky Relay

Eight Rainy Day Party Classics

1. Make a big bowl of popcorn and watch a favorite video.

2. Have a round-robin thumb-wrestling contest.

3. Hide pennies around the house and have the kids find them.

4. Make a paper doll chain.

5. Build a sofa cushion fort.

6. Play gin rummy.

7. Make paper airplanes and see whose model can fly the farthest.

8. Try to balance a spoon on your nose.

A Child's Tea Party

O NCE KIDS, especially little girls, discover the magical sound of china tinkling against china, setting up tiny cups and saucers often becomes a favorite pastime. That's why we pored over *FamilyFun* contributor Cynthia Caldwell's idea for her four-year-old daughter, Isabelle: an afternoon tea at which guests dress up in proper party fashion and get their fill of friendly chatter — and fancy finger foods.

Invitations to Tea

A TEA PARTY calls for invitations that look like fine china. For each one, cut out a colorful paper teacup and then use a gold or silver marker to outline the rim and handle. Print all the party particulars, along with a note that reminds guests that "Dolls and stuffed animals are welcome."

A Table Set for Tea

R EMEMBER, the fussier the table, the more the guests will like it. So, break out the ornate tablecloth, crocheted doilies, matching cups and saucers, and dessert dishes. Of course, you'll also need a teapot, a creamer, and a bowl of sugar cubes with tongs for serving one lump, or two. And don't forget to set places for teddy bears, too.

Teatime Activities

Sign In: Set out a feathered pen and a guest book (a small spiral-bound notebook with one of your child's drawings glued to the cover will suffice). Encourage each child to sign her name *and* her doll's.

Dress Up: Raid your closet for costume jewelry, old party dresses, gloves, and high heels. If you come up short, you can probably pick up a few inexpensive outfits at a thrift shop. Then let partygoers dress to the nines.

Make Dolls: Give each child an old-fashioned clothespin and lay out fabric scraps, lace, yarn, sequins, ribbons, and markers to make tiny fancy ladies to sit at the tea party table.

Silver Tea

It wouldn't be a tea party without a spot of tea. About five minutes before the guests are ready to be seated, steep a pot of decaffeinated tea. Then, to be sure the tea isn't too steaming hot, ask each child to fill her teacup halfway with milk before pouring. Add a spoonful of sugar and enjoy.

A Child's Tea Party

Tiny Tea Foods

Peanut Butter Pinwheels

Peanut Butter Pinwheels

Spread creamy or chunky peanut butter and a little bit of honey, fruit preserves, or apple butter on a fresh flour tortilla. Sprinkle with granola, roll up the tortilla, then slice it into bite-size pinwheels.

Shrunken Sandwiches

Shrunken Sandwiches

These cracker sandwiches are just the right size to share with stuffed animals. To make them, cut ham and cheese into small rounds. (You can use a clean bottle cap as a cutter to make it easy.)

Place ham rounds on the crackers, then the cheese. Cover each with another cracker.

Animal Cookies

Animal Cookies

For dessert, serve a plateful of sweet animals on parade. To make each one, you'll need three cookies of the same animal. Spread jam or peanut butter between them to make a three-layer filled cookie that will stand up on the serving dish.

Party Favors

BUY A CHILD's tea set and present one cup and saucer with a tea bag and a sugar cube to each guest. Or, give out candy jewelry, play makeup, and nail polish.

Sports Jamboree

PARTY STATS

Ages: 9 to 12
Size: 6 to 12 kids
Length: 2 to 4 hours
Prep time: 1 to 2 hours
Cost: $3 to $4 per guest

WITH QUICK BOUTS of football, basketball, and Wiffle ball to test your mettle, winning sports favors, and fare that's strictly ballpark, this bash is just the ticket for enthusiastic sports fans. It's also perfect for an end-of-the-season celebration for your child's athletic team. Your backyard or a nearby playground serves as the playing field, and the guests are the ballplayers.

Tag Football

Sports Invites

BEFORE YOU send out invitations, try to assess the athletic abilities of the guests in order to select two evenly matched teams that can compete throughout the party. "Draft picks" then can be announced on the invitations. To make the invitations, cut T-shirt shapes out of white paper. With crayons or markers (a different color for each team), accent the necklines and draw stripes above the hems. Then print the party details and a reminder for guests to dress for playing sports.

Decorations

BOLD BANNERS (in the teams' colors), pom-poms, and pennants make great pep rally props. You also can post a team roster on which sports fans can sign their names when they arrive — both their real ones *and* their sports nicknames of choice.

Play Ball

Tag Football: You'll need at least two kids on each team for this friendly, tamer version of big league football. The game begins as in tackle football, with a midfield lineup and kickoff. The receiving team attempts to run the ball back across the opponent's goal line to score a touchdown. Instead of tackling the player who's carrying the ball, members of the opposing team need only to tag him or her. If anyone is successful, play stops and the teams line up again where the runner was tagged. The team with the ball gets four chances (or downs) to score a touchdown before the ball passes to the other team.

Indoor Baseball

When her son, Michael, insisted that his sixth birthday party (which happened to be in November) reflect his passion for baseball, *FamilyFun* reader Rhonda Cloos of Austin, Texas, planned an indoor party that would keep her lamps intact. The boys pinned paper numbers to their jerseys, played Pin the Baseball in the Glove, and tossed a beanbag through a piece of poster board into which she had cut four bases.

Sports Jamboree

Sports Fan Favors

There's no striking out with these party favors: fill inexpensive baseball caps with whistles, sports cards, rubber balls, or chewing gum.

O-U-T! A day on the basketball court is not complete without a game of O-U-T (or any other word your kids want to spell). One player starts by shooting the ball from anywhere on the court. If it goes in, the other players must shoot from the same place (determine a shooting order in advance). Successful players are safe; those who miss get an O (the first letter of O-U-T). If the first player misses his first shot, the second player takes over the lead spot. Players must drop out when they get all letters of the chosen word; the last one in the game wins.

Chase the Dog: To join in this group game, each child will need a basketball and a bandanna tucked into a pocket (to resemble a tail). While staying within a designated area and continually dribbling their balls, players try to grab each other's bandannas. As soon as a player loses his tail, he is out. The game continues until only one child, the top dog, is left with his tail.

Three-Inning Baseball: For this mini match, follow the rules of traditional baseball with these exceptions: use a Wiffle ball and a plastic bat (no mitts needed) — and a lawn chair set up behind home plate in place of an umpire. The backrest defines the strike zone handily — if the ball hits it, it's a strike. Each team is at bat for just three innings.

Chase the Dog

Ballpark Menu

WHAT COULD BE better, or easier, to serve at a sports party than a classic ballpark lunch? For an extra treat, follow up with a dessert that's sure to score with kids: a cake that's shaped like a baseball cap.

Spicy Sports Popcorn

⅓ cup vegetable oil
1 cup popcorn kernels
1 1-ounce package taco seasoning mix
1 12-ounce jar unsalted dry-roasted
   peanuts

In a large pot, warm the vegetable oil over medium-high heat for a minute or two. Add the popcorn kernels. Cover and cook, shaking the pot, until the kernels stop popping.

Remove from the heat and pour half of the popcorn into a large paper bag. Add the taco seasoning and the peanuts. Add the remaining popcorn, fold over the top of the bag, shake, and serve. Makes about 20 cups.

Stadium Lunch

Serve grilled or steamed hot dogs and buns with mustard, catsup, or relish and cans of ice-cold soda.

Baseball Cap Cake

1 baked 8-inch round cake
1 dome cake (baked in a 1½-quart
   bowl or 6-inch sphere)
2 cups blue frosting
1 cup red frosting
   Red shoestring licorice
1 red gumdrop
   Red M&M's

Cut the 8-inch cake so that it is shaped like a brim and arrange it next to the bowl cake. Frost the hat blue and the brim red. Add shoestring licorice to the crown with a gumdrop button. Outline your child's initial in M&M's.

Baseball Cap Cake

Hot Seats

These sporty benchwarmer favors let party guests reserve cushy seats at the next big game. To make them, use a craft knife to cut handholds (adults only) in gardener's kneeling pads (sold at department stores for about $3). Let the kids print their names and slogans and draw sports symbols with permanent colored markers.

Backyard Camp-Out

PARTY STATS

Ages: All

Size: 4 to 20 guests

Length: Overnight

Prep time: 2 to 3 hours

Cost: $3 to $4 per guest

FAMILYFUN READER Rosemary Riccio and her Ward Hill, Massachusetts, neighbors shared their idea for an annual family camp-out, held in the Riccios' backyard. It's a time to swap ghost stories, roast marshmallows, and sleep under the stars. The party lasts just one night, but kids and adults alike look forward to it all year.

Good Green Camping

To make sure your camp-out is fun, safe, and environmentally friendly, follow these ground rules:

☛ Check the fire restrictions in your area, and never build a campfire unless it is in an established fire ring. Extinguish the fire *completely* by dousing the ashes with water.

☛ Burn only paper and wood — not plastic bottles, bags, or utensils.

☛ Put a lid on your trash by setting a garbage can and cover nearby.

Set Up Camp

A FUN WAY to start off a backyard camp-out is to turn the number one task — pitching tents — into a game. Divide into teams and see who can set up their tent the fastest.

Woodsy Vases

HAVE THE campers turn empty plastic jars into Woodsy Vases. Then they can fill them with wildflowers to spruce up the site for a camp-out feast. First gather a bunch of sticks (about ¼ inch in diameter). For each vase, snip the sticks to about 1 inch longer than the height of the jar you plan to use. Put two rubber bands around the jar, 1 inch from the top and bottom. Now tuck the sticks under both rubber bands, placing them as close as possible to each other. Once you've surrounded the jar with sticks, slide the rubber bands together at the jar's middle, then cover them with a decorative bow.

Campfire Feast

IT DOESN'T TAKE long for kids to get the hang of campfire cooking — using green sticks and aluminum foil instead of pots and pans,

Woodsy Vase

and standing upwind of the smoke. And even if they make the most common mistakes, such as slightly burning the dough or charring the marshmallows, the food still tastes good.

Camp Dough

Make a batch of this basic biscuit dough mix ahead of time and store it in a sealable plastic bag. During the camp-out, the kids can add water, mix, and use the dough to make Pups in a Blanket or Snakes on a Stick.

> ¼ cup margarine
> 2 cups all-purpose flour
> 3 tablespoons cultured buttermilk powder
> 1½ teaspoons cream of tartar
> ½ teaspoon baking soda
> ¾ cup water

In a large bowl, grate the margarine into the dry ingredients and mix until it resembles a coarse meal. Store the mixture in a sealable plastic bag and write "add ¾ cup water" on the out-side. To mix up the dough, pour the water into the bag and stir (do not add too much or overmix). Makes 2½ cups.

Pups in a Blanket

Camp-out guests will get a kick out of using Camp Dough to wrap around their hot dogs. For "cheese pups," first wrap the dog with a slice of American cheese.

> 1 hot dog
> 1 fist-size clump of Camp Dough or premade biscuit dough

For best results, slightly cook the hot dog before you wrap it with dough. You can heat it either on a thin forked stick

Pups in a Blanket

Backyard Camp-Out

over the campfire or in a piece of foil on the coals for 2 to 4 minutes. Meanwhile, flatten the dough into a thin rectangle that is long enough to wrap around the hot dog. Once the meat has cooled enough to handle, wrap the dough around it and then return it to the heat. Rotate the pup until the dough is cooked through.

Snakes on a Stick

A true kid favorite, this campfire biscuit treat is a snap to make. Begin with a green stick, about 2 feet long and ½ inch in diameter. Peel the bark off one end and briefly heat the end over the fire. Roll a fist-size clump of Camp Dough (you also can use premade biscuit dough) into a long, thin snake shape and carefully twist it around the peeled stick. Pinch the dough ends so the snake doesn't fall off the stick. Roast it over the fire until brown and cooked through, then slip it off the stick to eat.

Deluxe S'mores

Deluxe S'mores

A cookout wouldn't be complete without s'mores. To make one, sandwich a toasted marshmallow and a piece of chocolate between two graham crackers. Then try variations by putting pieces of the kids' favorite candy bars and toasted marshmallows between cookies or saltines.

Trail Mix

This classic camp snack is just right for satisfying the late-night munchies. For each camper, fill a sealable plastic bag with one of the following varieties.

Sunflower Seed Gorp: Combine 2 cups raw sunflower seeds and 1 cup each of pine nuts, raw pumpkin seeds, raisins, and sweetened dried cranberries.

Rain Forest Munch: Mix together 1 cup each of dried pineapple bits, dried papaya pieces, coconut flakes, macadamia nuts, cashews, and chocolate chunks.

Sweet and Salty Trail Mix: Mix 1 cup each of banana chips, M&M's, raisins, peanuts, pretzel sticks, and Goldfish.

Campfire Feast

Deluxe S'mores

With just a flashlight and their hands, campers can cast shadow creatures on the tent walls. Here are a few from *The Little Book of Hand Shadows* (Running Press).

Talking Horse: Clap your hands together, then lift up your thumbs and wiggle your pinkies.

Toothy Crocodile: Touch your wrists together and curl your fingers to create a crocodile's mouth.

Spider Crab: Cross your hands at the wrists, crook your thumbs, and wiggle your fingers.

Flashlight Fun

IT TAKES LITTLE more than a crackling campfire and a starlit sky to set the mood for a camp-out. Add a flashlight, and you've got instant, nightlong entertainment. (Just remember fresh batteries.)

Flashlight Freeze Tag: Select a pathway or an open area near the campsite for a playing area. One child — the night watcher — sits midway along the chosen path with his eyes closed and with a flashlight in hand. The other players start on one side of the path and try to sneak past the night watcher.

If the night watcher thinks someone is passing, he shines the light directly at the suspected spot. If the beam touches the player, she is frozen. Play continues until all of the sneakers are frozen, or you can start another round with the last player who was frozen as the new night watcher.

Send Flashlight Morse Code Signals: Pack a pocket encyclopedia or dictionary that includes the complete dot and dash code for reference. Campers can take turns trying to flash messages to one another on the tent ceiling.

Tell Glow-in-the-Dark Ghost Stories: No camp-out is complete without a few scary stories. When it's each storyteller's turn, she can hold a flashlight under her chin to give her face a creepy glow.

Slumber Party

ASK ANY GROUP OF GIRLFRIENDS: you just can't beat a chance to hang out in your pj's and chat all night long. The good news for parents is that with a few activities like the ones that follow and *lots* of munchies, a sleep-over generally throws itself. So, if you do lose sleep, it won't be over keeping the kids entertained.

Invitations

MINI PAPER pillows make cute invitations for a sleep-over party. For each one, cut a pair of 4¼- by 3-inch rectangles from white stationery. On one, print the party specifics and a reminder to bring a sleeping bag and pillow (you might add whether dinner is part of the party). Glue a couple of cotton balls to the center of the matching rectangle. Then glue the two rectangles together.

Nail Painting

ONCE THE GIRLS have arrived, they can catch up on all the news while they brush up on the latest in fingernail fashion. Here's a handful of designs for inspiration. One tip: A tiny watercolor brush (size 00) is great for detailing.

Plaid: Apply a base coat of polish. Once dry, add lines of a different color.

Starry Night: Top a dark undercoat with a glittery gold star.

Checkerboard: Start with a coat of red. Add staggered rows of black squares.

Pot of Gold: Paint a miniature rainbow at the tip of the nail.

Tiger Stripes: Apply an orange or gold undercoat. Add irregular black stripes.

Flower Garden: Top a base coat of green with daisies or tulips.

Polka Dots: Apply a base coat of polish. Dab on drops of another color.

Cow: Paint the nail white, then top with big black patches.

Lightning Bolt: Top a blue base coat with a bright yellow zigzag.

Red Delicious: Paint on a tiny apple complete with a stem and leaves.

Nail Painting

Rag Rolling

Rag Rolling

AFTER THE GIRLS dress in their pajamas, they can try this old-time hairstyling technique that will take them from rags to ringlets.

1. Tear fabric scraps into thin strips (8 to 10 inches long).

2. Using a spray bottle filled with water, dampen a guest's hair and comb out any knots.

3. Starting at the top of her head, lift a section of wet hair and place a fabric strip across its end. Roll the hair and the rag toward the scalp, then tie together the ends of the rag roller in a bow.

4. Repeat step 3, working down the back and sides, until the entire head of hair is rolled in rags. Leave the rollers in overnight.

5. In the morning, untie and unwind the rag rollers to unveil a headful of curls.

Slumber Party

Activities for Night Owls

◆ Pop in a dance lesson video and learn how to line dance or do the Macarena together.

◆ Braid embroidery floss into friendship bracelets or mix and match beads from old jewelry to make new necklaces.

Scrapbook

Scrapbook

THIS PASS-AROUND scrapbook lets sleep-over guests do what they love best: discuss what's cool. Each page is dedicated to a topic on which kids can share their opinions. Make one for each child, and they double as mementos of the big night.

For each book, you'll need a spiral sketchbook or a few sheets of unlined paper with holes punched along the side and bound together with ribbon.

Ask your child to print a different heading on each page, such as Our Favorite Animals, Best Movie, or Most Popular Saying. She can even pose a question, for instance, "What do you want to be when you grow up?" Next, divide each page into equal sections, one for each child to write in.

When the guests arrive, hand out the books and set out a bunch of colored markers everyone can use to jot down or draw their answers in each other's books.

Sleep-Over Cake

Since slumber parties aren't really about sleeping, let your wide-awake partygoers decorate cookies to look like their own faces, then tuck them into this sweet bed.

> 1 baked 13- by 9- by 2-inch cake
> 6 cups frosting (pink and light pink)
> Twinkies, marshmallows, and vanilla or chocolate wafers (1 for each guest)
> Gel icing (pink and green) and mini jawbreakers
> Pink and green Fruit by the Foot

Turn the cake upside down and lightly frost it. Cut the Twinkies in half lengthwise and center the tops, cut-side down, on the cake. Frost a pink sheet on the upper third of the cake. Flatten the marshmallows for pillows and place them above each Twinkie. Decorate the wafers (curly hair and big smiles can be made with gel icing; mini jawbreakers are perfect for eyes) and place the faces on the pillows. Frost a light-pink blanket over the Twinkies and the rest of the cake. Add gel icing flowers and a ruffled Fruit by the Foot bed skirt.

Slipper Socks

Slipper Favors

THESE ZANY Slipper Socks make a great slumber party craft. Each child gets to paint her own pair with bold, colorful designs. Then, left to dry overnight, they're ready to slip on the next morning.

To make each pair, you'll need cotton socks (pre-wash and dry them ahead of time, but do not use fabric softener), cardboard, a pencil, scissors, and nontoxic three-dimensional fabric paint. The paint, which is sold at most craft or fabric stores, comes in a variety of colors and costs about $3 for a 1-ounce bottle.

Have each child set her shoes on top of a piece of cardboard and trace around them with a pencil. Cut out the two shoe shapes with the scissors. Then fit the cardboard feet into a pair of the cotton socks so that they are pressed flat against the soles of the socks.

Now the kids can paint stars, fish, letters, or any other designs they like on the sock bottoms. Most three-dimensional paints can be applied straight from the bottle — just press the nozzle gently against the fabric to make sure the paint sticks.

Let the paint set overnight before removing the cardboard and wearing the slippers. You'll also want to wait about three days before you machine-wash and dry them (refer to the bottle for the proper heat settings).

Breakfast Sundaes

The morning after, tempt sleepyheads to rise and shine with fresh fruit sundaes. In parfait glasses, layer sliced peaches, bananas, melon, berries, and plain or flavored yogurt. Top with granola or finely chopped nuts and a cherry.

Playground Party

A SK KIDS WHAT'S the best part of school, and their answers are likely to be the same — recess. In this playground party, the whistle won't call everyone in before the fun is over. The following playground games require little supervision and less equipment — just rope, bottle caps, chalk, and a liberal dose of high spirits. So head to your local blacktop and listen for the happy sounds of kids calling the shots.

PARTY STATS

Ages: 6 to 8
Size: 6 to 12 kids
Length: 2 to 4 hours
Prep time: 2 hours
Cost: $2 to $4 per child

Invitation

F OR INVITATIONS, cut black construction paper into cards. Have your child decorate the cards with chalk drawings (of a hopscotch game or basketball court, for example). Write all the party details — including directions to the playground.

Spiral Hopscotch

B EGIN YOUR party with a recess game everyone knows the rules to: hopscotch. Instead of drawing the traditional board, sketch a spiral-shaped track of consecutive boxes (see photo at left). Give each player an equal number of bottle caps. To start, each player puts one cap on the square of his or her choice — and initials the square in chalk. The first player gets to shoot one of her caps (flicking it with her thumb, marbles style) and try to claim an empty spot or knock another player's cap off the board. If you knock a cap out, it's yours. And so is the space — everyone else will have to hopscotch over it. Rub out the previous player's chalk initials with your shoe and write in your own. If you flick your cap onto a marked space (without knocking that player's cap out), you lose your cap to that player.

The first player keeps shooting until she misses, then she must jump the course, staying off her opponents' squares. The next player shoots until he misses and then jumps the course, and so on. As the game progresses, more squares become off-limits, and longer hops are necessary. You're out of the game when you run out of caps. The player who takes over the whole board or winds up with all the caps wins.

Spiral Hopscotch

Airport

Airport

PICTURE CHICAGO'S O'Hare International Airport on a Monday morning. It may be one of the busiest airport on the planet, but it's nothing compared to the sheer mayhem this game can produce at your party. First, set up a "runway," an open space about 20 yards long and 6 to 8 feet wide. Mark it off with a stick in the dirt, with chalk on pavement, or with sticks or stones on grass.

One player, called the pilot, stands at the beginning of the runway and gets blindfolded. Her partner, the air traffic controller, stands at the far end of the runway. It is foggy, and the pilot must land her plane with help only from the air traffic controller. The pilot can move, but cannot see. The controller can see, but cannot move.

All the other players remove an article of clothing or grab a couple of things from their backpacks: sneakers, bulky sweaters, notebooks, soccer balls, tennis rackets, jump ropes, or basically anything else that isn't sharp or breakable. The players throw these objects onto the runway and leave them where they land, thus creating an obstacle course. The pilot must walk the course, arms outstretched like airplane wings, guided just by the controller's voice: "Okay, okay, two steps forward, but —

stop! Little steps! Step to the side now — no, to the other side. Watch out for the shin guards ... wait!"

If the pilot "crashes," she must either start over at the beginning of the runway or let another team take a turn. If she reaches the end of the runway, the blindfold is removed, and everyone applauds. Then it's another team's turn.

Chalk Your Walk

One of the playground's perks is that artists have a roomy canvas for their drawings — why else was asphalt invented? Here are some offbeat ways the party guests can decorate the blacktop with chalk. ◆ Draw a bird's-eye view of your town, complete with roads, houses, and parks. Then raid the playroom and populate it with toy cars and figures. ◆ Outline a huge sea serpent, dragon, or mythical beast and let partygoers each color in one section. ◆ Copy a favorite comic strip in the sidewalk squares (a panel in each square), or invent an original strip of your own. ◆ Play games like hangman or tic-tac-toe. ◆ Have one child create a connect-the-dots picture for another to complete.

Playground Party

Play Ball

Whether you're playing dodgeball, four-square, kickball, or spud, a playground party wouldn't be complete without a big red ball. Unlike basketballs, these soft rubber balls are kinder and gentler than basketballs, which means no one will end up in the school nurse's office.

Jump the Trap

WHIRLIGIG, Superlemon, Tightrope, Land Mine: whatever you call it, this has to be the simplest game ever invented — and one of the most fiendishly difficult to get really good at. It's fast-paced, easy to play, and requires kids to do one of their favorite things: jump!

To play, tie somebody's shoe to the end of a rope. (Kids have also been known to use a particularly detested textbook in place of the shoe. Social studies works well.) One player holds the shoeless end of the rope and spins around — not too fast — so that the rope sweeps in a circle. The weight keeps the rope fairly near the ground.

Players must jump over the rope as it passes them (this is easiest if kids spread themselves around the circle so they're not all in one clump). If the shoe hits a player's foot or leg, he's out. The last person still jumping gets to turn the rope during the next round.

Jump Rope Rhymes

TALLY UP HOW many times players can jump rope without missing by using a rhyming jingle. For instance, they might chant "Candy, candy in a dish. How many pieces do you wish?" then count "One, two, three," and so on, until the jumper misses.

Jump the Trap

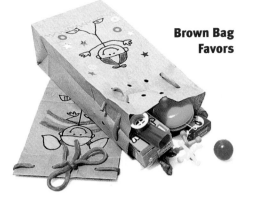

Brown Bag Favors

Brown Bag Lunch & Favors

A PLAYGROUND PARTY calls for a paper bag lunch — and this one comes with a prize. Before the party, decorate paper lunch bags with drawings, ribbons, and stickers. Then fill them with half a PB & J and half a cheese sandwich, along with pretzels, carrot sticks, raisins, dessert, and a juice box. Stuff each bag with a party favor: a jump rope, a Hackey Sack, a chalk pack, or a set of jacks.

Hopscotch Cake

A SSEMBLING THIS CAKE is only half the fun. When it's ready to serve, kids can take turns standing a short way from the end of the cake and tossing a piece of candy or cereal onto it. The "tosser" gets to eat the slice of cake on which his marker lands.

> 1 13- by 9- by 2-inch baked cake
> 2 cups frosting
> Decorations: shoestring licorice, colored sugar, mini candies, fruit leather, and shredded coconut

Cut the cake into eight rectangular pieces and arrange the pieces on a board or serving tray in the classic hopscotch pattern. Frost the cake. To deco-

rate it, snip licorice strings and use them to mark the rectangles. Make numbers on each rectangle with frosting, mini candies, colored sugar, or pieces of fruit leather. Jazz up the hopscotch squares with more candies and colored sugar or shredded coconut.

Hopscotch Cake

**Family Olympics,
page 122**

Chapter Four

Crowd Pleasers

Cool-Off Party ★ Block Party ★ All-Star Carnival
Beach Party ★ Family Olympics ★ Fall Festival
Skating Party ★ A Snow Ball

EVERY YEAR, *FamilyFun* contributor Charlotte Meryman and her family welcome spring with a big, boisterous bash. And every year, the party gets a little bigger — and better. Last year, nearly 100 guests (half kids and half adults) gathered the weekend after Memorial Day on her Massachusetts farm for an old-fashioned day of fun, games, and food that lasted long after dark.

Large gatherings, like Charlotte's annual bash, do take a lot of planning. To throw a successful big party, she says, you need to start with a basic game plan that has something for everyone — games, activities, and food for all ages. Once the guests arrive, Charlotte lets the party take on a life of its own. The best moments, she says, are often unexpected.

In this chapter, we've featured eight parties that please a mixed-age crowd of 20 to 100 guests. If you're up for hosting a big bash, start by choosing one of our party plans that appeals to your family's tastes, from the wintry Snow Ball on page 138 to the All-Star Carnival on page 112. Once you have settled on a theme, mix and match ideas from other parties and toss in your own unique twists (asking key guests for input).

Admittedly, large events take more effort, but they also have a greater payoff. Charlotte loves it when people start asking about her party months ahead of time. She says, "I know we're creating the kind of memories I treasure from my own childhood."

Start early: Allow several weeks to several months for at-home parties. If you need to book a space elsewhere or if guests will be traveling from out of

Beach Ball Invitation, page 118

Crowd Pleasers

Family Reunions

No matter how connected we are in today's information age, there's nothing like seeing your family face to face. Any of the parties in this chapter can be adapted to suit a large family gathering. Use an entire theme, such as the Family Olympics on page 122, or a mix of games and activities from this chapter.

town, start planning six months ahead.

Set a date: Notify guests right away for a good turnout. For annual events, establish a permanent date, such as the first Saturday in May. Resist the temptation to reschedule, no matter how many regrets you receive. (If there are guests you consider essential, check with them early.) For weather-dependent events, set an alternate date, too.

Spread the work around: A good host knows how to delegate. Make a list of the tasks that need to be done (including deadlines), from the invitations to the menu to the cleanup. Then divvy up the responsibilities with members of your family or a party committee. Check in regularly and reassign jobs that aren't getting done.

Plan activities for all ages: Soliciting ideas from people of varying ages will help ensure that there are activities to satisfy everyone. Plan an icebreaker, such as a group game, early in the party to help draw guests together and get the party rolling.

Arrange for child care: Hiring a few neighborhood teens to entertain toddlers can make the party more fun for them and give their parents a chance to participate in the activities.

Make the food potluck: Not only are potlucks the easiest meal to prepare, but they have the added advantage of giving guests a chance to contribute. If someone makes a dish you've enjoyed in the past, consider requesting it again; you'll probably find they're more than happy to oblige.

Don't forget to document: Stock up on film before the party and assign a few "photographers," or hand out disposable cameras. A group shot is a terrific way to remember the day.

Write it all down: Take advantage of the inevitable post-party review to jot down notes for next year's bash, such as how many people attended, what they consumed, and where and when the supplies were rented, plus note any great ideas from guests.

Skating Party, page 132

Cool-Off Party

PARTY STATS

Ages: All
Size: 10 to 20 guests
Length: 2 to 4 hours
Prep time: 2 hours
Cost: $3 per guest

WHEN IT'S 90 DEGREES in the shade, don't sweat it out alone. Lure friends and family away from their air conditioners and over to your house for a rollicking cool-off party. What follows are water games, cold foods, and favorite tricks that will leave everyone smiling, splashing, and feeling as cool as cukes.

A Hot Spot

THE MOST IMPORTANT thing you'll need for this party is sizzling hot weather, so plan on hosting it in the heat of the summer. Choose a date (and a rain date) and invite a bunch of kids and their parents via telephone. If you aren't lucky enough to have a pool in your backyard, plan the party at a public swimming area, pool, or lake. Alternatively, ask guests to bring their own wading pools and create a big pool party in your backyard. No matter where you host the event, you'll want to haul out the pool toys, water balloons, and squirt guns, then get ready to dive right into the coolest celebration around.

Crowd Pleasers

Splash Tag

Cool-Off Party

Cool Pool Competitions

- ☞ Dive for a penny at the pool bottom
- ☞ Throw an underwater tea party
- ☞ Hold a chat at the bottom of the pool
- ☞ Do a cartwheel underwater
- ☞ Grab a greased watermelon
- ☞ Style a wet and wacky hairdo

Musical Sprinkler

IN THIS AQUATIC adaptation of statue, a sprinkler takes the place of music. One great thing about the game is that everyone is a winner, because everyone gets cool. Begin play with the sprinkler turned off. Players must move around the sprinkler area, jumping, dancing, or striking funny poses. When the sprinkler is turned on, they must freeze in position — and get drenched — until the sprinkler is turned off again.

Musical Sprinkler

The Great Foot Freeze

The Great Foot Freeze

HERE'S A SILLY group icebreaker that will cool your guests off in a hurry. Fill a child's plastic wading pool with water, then add lots of ice cubes. Now supply each contestant with a plastic bowl. (All bowls should be roughly equal in size.) Players sit around the edge of the wading pool with their feet poised over the water. At the word "Go," they race to move ice cubes out of the water and into their bowls within a designated time period. The catch is, they can only use their feet. The winner — by a foot, of course — is the person who has the most ice cubes in his bowl when the time is up.

Foot Freeze is one game where kids have a distinct advantage over grownups: not only do their feet seem to be much more dexterous, kids also aren't nearly such wimps about plunging their toes into the (eek!) icy water.

Parent Polo

THEY SAY NOBODY knows you like your mother, but is that really the case? Just go to the grocery store and see how many women turn around when just one child cries "Mom!" In this variation of the classic pool game Marco Polo, first mothers and then fathers have to find their own children in the pool on the basis of voice alone. Parent Polo can be played in a swimming pool or lake; otherwise your only requirement is to have a lifeguard on duty to watch the kids.

When you're ready to play, have all the kids and their moms get into the pool. (In the second heat, it's the dads' turn to dive in.) Each parent closes his or her eyes, then the adults count to ten in unison while the kids spread out in the water (shallow end only, unless the kids are all strong swimmers), with siblings grouped together. The moms now begin to search for their own children by listening to their voices. Kids call out "Mommy!" and the moms must respond "Polo!" The first mom to touch her slippery kids wins. Follow with a round of Daddy Polo.

Parent Polo

Cool-Off Party

Water Volley Balloon

Water Volley Balloon

THE BIGGEST problem with beach volleyball is that you get so terribly hot playing it. To the rescue comes this cool twist on the game. And unlike regular volleyball, which requires no small degree of skill, this game doesn't favor natural athletes. To get underway, you'll need a volleyball or badminton net, two old sheets, and an ample supply of water balloons. Not to mention a group of party animals who don't mind getting all wet.

Divide players into two teams of four and have them stand on opposite sides of the net. Each team holds one sheet (a person at each corner). Place a water balloon in the center of one team's sheet. That team must use its sheet to toss the balloon over the net. It helps to do a countdown: "One, two, three . . . Up!" The other team then must catch the balloon in its sheet and toss it back from whence it came.

Depending on how much you feel like cooling off, winners can be the first team to make either ten catches or ten misses. Bonus points may be awarded for real soakers. Note to parents: This game is a hit with older kids, who run with the sheet, trying to guess where the balloon will land, but little kids may get yanked around. And broken balloons should be immediately retrieved, so that toddlers aren't tempted to see how they taste.

Splash Tag

ONE THING most kids will never learn to like about tag is being "It." All that pressure, all those elusive runners to catch. Somehow this particular variation reduces the stigma just a little bit. Maybe it has something to do with the sopping sponge the It player gets to wield in wet and wild Splash Tag. Or maybe it's just the way all the other players seem to run right up and beg to be tagged …

A big, soft sponge, like the kind you use to wash the car, and several buckets of frigid water are all the equipment you need to get started.

The game is played like straight tag, with everybody running from It and his big bad sponge. Once a player is hit, he or she becomes the new It. In Splash Tag there's no bickering about whether someone actually got tagged: it's pretty hard for anyone to make a convincing denial when his back is dripping wet.

Cold Potato

Splash Tag

Crowd Pleasers

Cold Potato

THIS SIMPLE game revolves around a sprinkler, but not the kind you're imagining. Instead of your garden-variety sprinkler, Cold Potato is played with a leaky water balloon.

To get going, prick a hole in a balloon with a safety pin. Then fill the balloon with cold water, so that it becomes a slowly leaking time bomb. Players stand in a circle and toss the balloon around. The object is to avoid being the person left holding the balloon when it runs out of water. To avoid being absolute drips, players must have quick reflexes and a good toss.

Swimsuit Cover-Ups

Kelly Smith of Cleveland, Tennessee, found a practical, and pretty, party favor by modifying an idea from *FamilyFun*. The kids decorated big T-shirts with handprint flowers, then painted on long green stems.

Cool-Off Party

Relative Relay

Relative Relay

FAMILIES GO for the gold in this Olympic-style swimming relay, which focuses more on the sillies than the strokes.

Line up all the families in the starting area (the race can be conducted in a pool, a lake, or a pond). If some families have more members than others, even out the teams. If possible, try to match dads against dads, moms against moms, kids against kids. Once you get your teams straightened out, you're ready to begin.

At a signal, the first member of each family dives in to swim a single lap. As soon as that person finishes, the next family member jumps in and swims hers, and so on, until the whole team has finished. The first family to complete all its laps wins.

The contest proceeds just like any other relay, really, except with one big catch: racers must perform a feat while swimming. For example, in lap one, all the moms must push beach balls across the pool using only their noses. In lap two, cousins must paddle on water noodles. For lap three, the grandmothers must frog-kick behind kickboards. In lap four, kids must dog-paddle while singing "Yankee Doodle." For the anchor lap, the dads must do the breaststroke with rubber ducks balanced on their heads. Make up your own rules. The zanier the better.

On the face of it, you might think that competitive swimmers would hold a decided advantage over their less aquatic friends in the Relative Relay. After all, this is a swimming contest, right? Not so fast. Ever try to do an expert backstroke when you're giggling hard enough to make waves in the pool? It ain't easy.

Cool Cuisine

EVERY HOST likes her guests to think her menu is cool, especially during a party such as this one. If it's really hot outside, your guests may not feel like eating at all, but make sure they stay hydrated with plenty of water and party drinks. If they do work up a hunger, offer them cold cuts to build their own sandwiches along with an Arctic Orange and a slice of Sunshine Cake.

Arctic Oranges

Arctic Oranges

4 oranges
4 cups orange juice
4 cherries, pitted
8 raisins
4 apple slices

Cut the tops off the oranges in a zigzag pattern. Hollow out the insides, remove the seeds, and combine in a blender with the juice. Set the rinds in a muffin tin and fill with the mixture. Drop a cherry inside each orange. Freeze for 2 to 3 hours. Use toothpicks

Sunshine Cake

Frozen Favors

to apply raisin eyes and apple slice mouths. Let the kids eat their way down to the surprise cherry. Makes 4.

Sunshine Cake

2 8- or 9-inch round baked cakes
Yellow frosting
7 to 9 sugar cones
Yellow crystal sugar

Frost the top of one cake, then add the second layer and continue frosting. Ice the outside of one cone and roll it in the sugar. Push the open end into the side of the cake, using more frosting to hold it in place, if needed. Repeat with the other cones, positioning them around the cake like sun rays. Serves 8 to 10.

Frozen Favors

Cap your cool-off party with this frosty favor. For each child, insert a small toy or piece of plastic jewelry into a balloon. Fill the balloon with water, knot it, and freeze solid. Before giving out the goodies, cut away the balloon. Now young guests can push the ice ball around a kiddie pool and watch it melt into a surprise.

Block Party

A BLOCK PARTY is your chance to move beyond the nodding acquaintance you may have with the people next door. When you serve up food and fun, you'll be swapping recipes and baby-sitters' phone numbers in no time. The following block party plan, sent in by the folks who live on Tucker Street in suburban Natick, Massachusetts, is one neighborhood's recipe for success.

Party Preparations

THE FIRST THING you need to do is solicit volunteers for a planning committee — this is not a project you want to tackle solo. The party chairman (a job that should be rotated every couple of years) must request, in advance, town permission to block off the street. Subcommittees can plot out food, games, and the much-anticipated variety show.

Mail Flyers

ONCE YOU HAVE settled on a date and time, invitations can be sent out (3 to 8 P.M. will ensure that dinner can be served around 5 o'clock followed by the talent show). Have a subcommittee member write out all the party info by hand or on a computer, then reproduce the invites at a copy shop. Now all you have to do is stuff them in the mailboxes.

Mail Flyer

The Kick-Off Parade

THIS EARLY afternoon event sets the mood for the later festivities. The kids proudly present their bikes, strollers, and wagons decorated with anything they can think of. Have plenty of decorations on hand, such as streamers, helium balloons, bows, and ribbons. Notch playing cards or slit straws down their sides and slip over wheel spokes. Tape pinwheels to the handlebars and watch the parade begin.

Rock Around The Block

ADD AN INSTRUMENTAL ambience to the day's activities by trying this idea provided by Robin Conti of Natick, Massachusetts. Tune radios up and down the block to a common station (chosen by committee, of course) and bring speakers outdoors or aim them out opened windows.

The Kick-Off Parade

Crowd Pleasers

Block Party

Cool-de-Sac Classics

Please the neighborhood gang with one of these tried-and-true classics:

- ☞ Horseshoes
- ☞ Croquet
- ☞ Badminton
- ☞ Wiffle ball
- ☞ Dodgeball (try kids versus parents)
- ☞ Lawn golf
- ☞ Red rover
- ☞ Kick the can

Fun & Games

Rowdy Races: At the Tucker Street block party, Robin said it was amusing to see how many of the men participated in the relay races. They actually had to have a separate men's division. Along with relays, try three-legged races (an adult class featuring married couples hobbling together is hysterical), wheelbarrow runs (one person holds up the legs of another person walking on his hands), and trash bag sack hops.

Lawn Mower Race: Dads will need little incentive or instruction to participate in this game. Simply line up riding or push mowers, stand back as engines roar, and point the contestants toward the grass.

Know Thy Neighbor: In this game, families find out how well they know the neighborhood. Hand out copies of a map of all the houses in the surrounding area and challenge players to fill in the names of who lives at each. At the end of the game, answers should be read aloud, so people can fill in any blanks. Add phone numbers, and the completed map now serves as an impromptu neighborhood directory.

Treasure Hunt: At the party planning stage, a subcommittee can be charged with thinking up the clever clues to lure family teams to a hidden pile of loot in the neighborhood. (For complete directions on staging treasure hunts, see page 19.)

Rowdy Races

Variety Show

Neighborhood Fun

There are more ways than one to throw a block party. Any of these ideas can be worked into your gathering.

Show Off Your Pets: Have kids present their loyal pals for prizes at the party — Most Bashful Guppy, Happiest Dog, Sleepiest Cat, and so on.

Watch a Movie: Rent a movie projector and play it on an outdoor screen — a white sheet hung on the side of the house. Alternatively, have neighbors bring a handful of slides from a favorite family vacation to share.

Catch Community Spirit: Add a can or clothing drive element to the block party — or make group plans for future volunteer projects.

Blockbuster Menu

TEN DOLLARS per family buys barbecue meats and drinks (and contributes to the rental of "military-size grills," as Robin puts it). One side of the street is charged with making salads, the other, desserts.

Variety Show

ONE OF LIFE'S great thrills is a stage curtain lifting — even if the curtain is a bedspread and the stage a bit grassy. To form an easy performance space at your block party, run a clothesline between two large trees and drape sheets over the line. Add a portable mike and a spotlight, and the show is ready to go on.

Before the party, have parents help kids find a particular talent they want to show off: Is it training the family dog? Doing impressions of her parents? Playing the kazoo? Bear in mind that the key to a successful show is raw enthusiasm and an appreciative audience, not polished performances.

Consider anchoring the show with one big number that involves the whole cast. This way, the kids will have an excuse to get together regularly for rehearsals before the party.

If you're long on neighborhood talent but short on plot ideas, take your script from stories the kids know. They can stick to the original or — for a fun twist — modernize or adapt it. What if Cinderella lived in the nineties or Clifford was a big, red cat?

Once the dinner dishes are cleared, let the talent show begin. For an extra touch and a souvenir of the event, have the kids pass out programs that have been made on a computer.

All-Star Carnival

GAMES, CONTESTS, PRIZES, music, sweets, and sunshine. Put them all together, and you get the most memorable event of the summer — a carnival. Whether you make it a neighborhood street fair or use a few ideas for a birthday party, the principle is the same: you dream up the festivities, then invite carnivalgoers to wander from booth to booth, playing games, trying their luck, and, well, clowning around.

Set Right Up

FOLLOW *FamilyFun*'s tried-and-true formula for throwing a carnival: keep things simple, sweet, and silly. You will need a group of willing friends and an open area (a field, backyard, or park) with access to a hose and faucet. Decide which booths and contests you want to set up, then choose a date and a rain date. Divvy up the planning and enlist kids to help with the booth-making and decorating — carnival construction is half the fun. Then put up a few carnival posters and wait for the eager crowds to pour in.

Ticket Booth

The Booths

THE BACKBONE of any carnival is an array of enticing booths. To make one, start with a bench, table, or cardboard box, then drape it with a bright tablecloth or sheet. Attach balloons, streamers, pinwheels, or flags, and, most importantly, a hand-painted sign listing the booth's name and the ticket fee. Staff each booth with an adult or teen attendant with a basket of prizes.

Ticket Booth: As an entrance fee to the big event, ask carnivalgoers to bring a donation of $1. (This pays for the prizes — penny candy, stickers, rubber balls, and other inexpensive toys.) When the donation is made, the booth manager hands out a paper bag with 20 tickets. Throughout the fair, kids can pay a ticket to enter an event. When they receive a prize, they can stow it in the bag.

Wet Sponge Toss: Armed with a garbage can lid, a valiant parent at this booth must defend himself or herself from kids who get three chances to make a direct hit with a large, wet sponge. Depending on the weather, parent volunteers can don rain gear or swimsuits. Provide a bucket of water and at least three thick, soft sponges and mark off a line behind which the

Wet Sponge Toss

assailants must stand. The target can duck, twist, or wield the shield to avoid the wet missiles — but must remain with feet planted as kids pitch. A hit wins the contestant a prize.

Guess Your Weight: Nothing pleases young carnivalgoers more than outsmarting a grown-up. Decked out in full academic regalia, a dad or mom masquerading as Professor Guesser must try to guess the weight of children who step up to his or her scale. If the professor's guess is within five pounds, the child wins nothing. If the guess is more than five pounds over or under, the child wins a prize. A full-size, stand-up scale lends drama to the game — but if Professor Guesser is enough of a natural-born ham, any size scale will do for this fun and suspenseful contest.

Guess Your Weight

Face-Painting

Ask an artistic teen to be in charge of face-painting the not-too-squirmy carnival attendees. Beforehand, buy a high-quality face paint kit, such as Professional Snaz-aroo Face Painting Kit, which is available at department and party stores for about $15. Then paint faces with stars, flowers, rainbows, hearts, clown noses, or animal stripes.

All-Star Carnival

Ready, Aim, Fire!

Guess the Joke

At fourth grader Katie Clark's carnival in Jackson, Michigan, kids paid a ticket for a chance to get lucky ... with laughter. Booth attendants got out their joke books, wrote down their favorites, then put all the questions in a hat. For a ticket, carnival revelers got to pull one out and try to guess the punch line. If they guessed right, they received a prize. Stumped? They got a consolation prize — and a good laugh when they heard the answer.

Ready, Aim, Fire! Players in this throwing contest will need a strong arm and a sense of aim that is right on the money. To set the stage, use pieces of string or twine to hang a series of targets from a long tree branch or a clothesline. Make your targets a variety of shapes and sizes, using paper plates, aluminum pie pans, hula hoops, beach balls, wind chimes, cowbells, spinning targets, or anything else you can think of. Label each target, indicating how many prizes a successful hit is worth (anywhere from one to four, depending on the difficulty), then mark off a line 10 to 15 feet away. Each contestant pays a ticket, steps up to the line, and gets three tennis balls — and three chances to try her luck on any of the targets.

Speedy Delivery: For a ticket, kids can send a surprise (a balloon? jelly beans? a lollipop?) to a parent or pal. After picking a prize and writing an accompanying note, the gift-giver can sneak to the sidelines to watch as a courier, decked in a sandwich board, delivers the surprise with a flourish.

Penny Splash: This event requires an aquarium filled with water, two or three tall glasses, and a bowl filled with pennies. Set the aquarium on a sturdy table and sink the glasses so they sit upright on the bottom of the tank. Contestants then try to drop pennies into the glasses. Award a prize for every lucky penny that makes its mark.

Speedy Delivery

The Contests

WHAT'S A GOOD carnival without a few sporting events? Next to the ticket booth, set up a poster listing all the contests, their locations, and their starting times (you may want to run a number of heats throughout the carnival so that everyone can participate). When kids arrive, they can sign up for one or all of the contests, then meet at the appointed spot at game time. An adult or teen can monitor each event, explaining the rules and making sure the competition stays fair and friendly.

Outrageous Obstacle Course: For this game, two relay teams race through identical obstacle courses — the first team that completes its run wins. The obstacle course at your

Outrageous Obstacle Course

carnival can be as wild as your imagination and resources permit, but here are a few ideas to start with. Racers can crawl through hula hoops, bounce balls, step in and out of tires, jump over a sleeping alligator (a hay bale), step into a sack and jump a few yards, shoot a water gun, or pitch a Frisbee disc through a hoop. When each runner has completed the obstacles, she must run backward (not through the course) and tag the next runner on her team. The winning team gets a prize apiece.

Balloon Stomp: This event requires a few packages of medium-size round balloons, string, lots of eager participants, and a small field marked off with cones. Competitors should blow up two balloons and tie one to each ankle. The object is to stomp other people's balloons while keeping yours intact. The judge yells "Go!" and all players start stomping, remaining on the field at all times. The last person to remain unpopped wins a prize — and the right to pop her own balloon.

Spin & Run: Absurdity rules the day in this game, which requires nothing but a bunch of baseball bats and a finish line. To play, each contestant must grip a bat and hold it upright so the top rests on the ground. Then players must bend over, place their foreheads on the ends of the bats, and spin around ten times. After this, they drop the bats and attempt to race for the finish line (a more difficult task than you might expect). Don't play with too many kids or you'll have to rename it Spin & Collide.

Spin & Run

All-Star Carnival

Water Balloon Toss

Water Balloon Toss: Here, kids try to toss water-filled balloons to each other over increasing distances without breaking them. Have pairs of kids face each other in a line and give one child in each pair a filled balloon. On the starting whistle, the child must toss the balloon to her partner. If her partner can catch the balloon without breaking it, both children take a step backward. On the next whistle, the sequence is repeated. If a balloon bursts, that pair of kids is eliminated. The pair that can toss its balloon from the greatest distance wins a prize.

Cracker Whistling: The familiar schoolyard expression "Say it, don't spray it" definitely does not apply to this silly contest. In fact, players must whistle a simple tune even though they have a mouthful of crackers. To set up the contest, you will need a table, chairs, small paper plates, and a couple of boxes of crackers. Seat each contestant in front of a plate with two crackers. At the starting whistle, players must chew as quickly as they can, then try to be the first one to whistle a few bars of a specified tune for a prize. Have a few glasses of water handy and — a word to the wise — stand clear.

Bucket Brigade: This race requires two evenly numbered teams, one bucket for each player, a filled wading pool with a running hose inside it, and two washtubs (or trash cans) with a tennis ball tossed into each. Team members must coordinate the fastest method for filling their washtubs with buckets of water. The first group to make the tennis ball spill out of the tub wins.

Cracker Whistling

The Food Booth

With the scent of barbecue in the air, contestants will converge on this booth quickly. Cover a table with a cloth and set out plates, utensils, condiments, and a cooler of drinks. Place a grill nearby and let the chef du jour preside over hot dogs and hamburgers (charge 10 tickets for dogs, 20 tickets for burgers, and 5 tickets for juice boxes or soda). For dessert, set up a decorate-your-own-cupcake table, where kids can indulge a sweet tooth with frostings and sprinkles for 5 tickets.

The Toddler Corner

TREAT THE YOUNGEST carnival-goers to a play area with games and contests that are just their speed (older siblings and parents are admitted by toddler invitation only). Station a few parents or teens to collect tickets, run the fun and games, and hand out a prize to each child who completes an event.

Doll Show

Music-Makers Tent

Music-Makers Tent: Here, a magical tent sets the stage for dressing up and making music. Dolled up in play clothes, hats, and paper leis, kids can pound on drums, tootle on harmonicas, rattle maracas, and dance the day away. Pitch a camping tent, set out the supplies, and let the kids make some noise.

Tricycle Races: Soup up a few three-wheeled hot rods with streamers and bows, and the racers will be lining up for a chance to pedal to victory. Make a finish line by hanging crepe paper between two poles and use traffic cones or milk jugs weighted with sand to delineate the racecourse.

Doll Show: For this event, little children get to dress up one of their favorite dolls or stuffed animals. They bring along their dolls, and you provide a box of doll clothes, ribbons, bows, and hairbrushes. After thoroughly primping

and adorning their charges, the kids can parade before a panel of friendly judges. Every contestant's entry receives a prize — for fanciest dress, funniest hat, cutest smile, longest hair, fuzziest fur, or best button nose.

Bubble Factory: When little kids see bubbles flying through the air, they'll flock to this event. Fill pie plates with store-bought bubble soap and hand out a selection of wands, from giant bubble makers to mini wands.

Edible Jewelry: This activity combines two all-time favorites: stringing beads and eating sweets. Offer kids Fruit Loops and shoestring licorice and let them string themselves an edible necklace.

Art Show: For a kids' carnival mural, hang a roll of newsprint from a clothesline or tape it to a garage door and offer paint and brushes (keep a hose nearby for cleanup!).

Tricycle Races

Carnival Booths for Little Kids

Magnet Fishing: Stock a dry kiddie pool with paper fishes with paper clips attached to their mouths. Let kids fish with a magnet tied to a fishing pole.

Lucky Lollipop: Stick lollipops in a Styrofoam cone. For a ticket, kids get to pull one out. If it has a red mark on the end, they win a prize; if not, the lollipop itself is a happy consolation.

Dig for Buried Treasure: Bury hidden treasures (inexpensive prizes) in a sandbox. One ticket lets kids dig until they discover a prize.

Tire Target: Hang an old tire from a tree and let kids try to toss a football through it.

Beach Party

T HE SEASHORE — with the waves rolling in, the cloudless sky, the gulls winging overhead — offers a picturesque setting for a family party. Young shell-seekers will find plenty to do, from decorating sand castles to playing tic-tac-toe, while their parents drink in the view from beach chairs. All the activities can take place right on a public beach. Best of all, the party favors begin with a pocketful of beach finds.

PARTY STATS

Ages: All
Size: 10 to 20 guests
Length: 2 to 4 hours
Prep time: 2 hours
Cost: $4 to $6 per guest

Beach Ball Invitations

T HE IDEA of a day at the beach should be inviting enough, so get guests in the party mood with a beach ball invitation. Inflate inexpensive plastic beach balls and use a permanent marker to write down the party info. Ask guests to pack their beach bags with towels, bathing suits, beach chairs, and sunscreen. Deflate the balls and send in manila envelopes.

Beach Ball Invitation

Shell T-Shirts

A S GUESTS ARRIVE, invite them to print summery designs with seashells on white T-shirts or tank tops. Place newspaper inside the T-shirts to keep the paint from leaking through. Next pour fabric paint onto a sponge. Press the outside of a shell into the paint and then onto the shirt. Repeat, experimenting with different colors. At home, guests should heat-set the paint according to package directions.

Shell T-shirts

Sand Sculpture Contest

T HE KIDS at your beach party will probably take one quick plunge in the water, bounce around in the surf for about 30 seconds, then want to spend the rest of the afternoon digging sand sculptures on the beach. So why not stage a Sand Sculpture Contest as the focal point of the party?

Keep the contest rules straightforward: a sculpture can be made with any available tools or materials — driftwood, shells, beach pails, plastic shovels, even boogie boards — and it should represent the collaborative efforts of a family or parent-child team. Sand sculptures might include a dune buggy (like the one pictured at right), a sea lion with a seaweed mane, or a motorboat with a (real) waterskiing dad getting towed behind.

Award prizes for the goofiest, most artistic, sandiest, and most creative use of beach finds. For prizes, present disposable underwater cameras or plastic sunglasses.

Sand Sculpture Contest

Beach Party

Beach Bowling

Beach Hunt

Send teams of beach-combers on a scavenger hunt. Depending on where you live, the list might include:

- ☞ **Blue sea glass**
- ☞ **Driftwood**
- ☞ **10 types of shells**
- ☞ **A sand dollar**
- ☞ **3 types of seaweed**
- ☞ **8 smooth sea stones**
- ☞ **A crab or starfish**
- ☞ **10 pieces of trash**
- ☞ **A found penny**
- ☞ **A snail**

Note: Remind kids to return living things to their natural habitat.

Beach Games

Musical Towels: Lay out beach towels — one fewer than players — on the sand and turn up the music on a portable stereo (we recommend the Beach Boys or any surfer sounds). When the music starts, players dance around the towels. When it stops, players must stretch out on a towel like a sunbather. The player left without a towel is out. Remove one towel each round until there's only one remaining beach bum.

Beach Bowling: First, build ten pins by filling a cup with moist sand. Carefully turn the cup over and lift it off. Set up the pins in a triangle with one pin in front, two pins in the next row, three in the next, and four in the back row.

Next draw a starting line in the sand about 6 or 8 feet from the pins. Now take turns standing behind the line and rolling a softball or other small ball toward the pins to knock them over. Each player gets to roll the ball twice. Count how many pins you knock over, set them up again, and keep score in the sand.

Tic-tac-toe: Make a nine-square grid in the sand and draw the X's and O's with driftwood. If you have enough partygoers who want to play, make teams and ask human markers to sit in the squares.

Hopscotch: To give this playground classic a seaside flavor, each player can scavenge a beach-related marker to toss: a clamshell, a plastic shovel, or a colorful flip-flop.

Darts: Draw a dartboard with six concentric circles and give each ring a point value. Each player should choose three markers that look the same (three clamshells, three pieces of green sea glass, and so on). Take turns tossing the markers at the dartboard and keep score in the sand.

Beach Bowling

Sandy Food

PACK A COOLER with juice boxes and bottled water — and a variety of picnic salads and sandwiches. For a sweet surprise, bring along the Pail of Sand Cake (below).

Seashore Snacks

For a party snack mix, fill a large paper bag with 1 cup each of dry chow mein noodles (seaweed), pretzel sticks (driftwood), Cheddar Goldfish crackers, roasted peanuts (beach pebbles), and Cheerios (life preservers). For sweetness, add 1 cup of raisins and ½ cup of dried pineapple slices cut into bite-size wedges. Fold over the top of the bag and shake to mix.

Pail of Sand Cake

This novel cake, topped with crushed cookie "sand," will be the hit of your beach party. After your kids eat it up, scrub the pail and let them fill it with real sand (no eating allowed).

> 1 baked 8-inch round cake
> 1 8- to 9-cup capacity new plastic sand pail
> 24 ounces unsweetened applesauce (or 1 3-ounce package pudding, prepared)
> ¾ cup crushed graham crackers or vanilla cookies
> Shell candies
> 1 plastic shovel

Cut the cake into 1-inch pieces. Fill the pail, alternating layers of cake pieces and applesauce, ending with applesauce. Sprinkle on the crushed cookie sand and top with shell candies. Now dig in with the plastic shovel.

Indoor Beach Party

Being snowed in is just another day at the beach for *FamilyFun* reader Cathy Rickarby of Stratham, New Hampshire. When her kids had a snow day from school, they hosted an indoor beach party. While Cathy packed lunch in a cooler, Carly, age five, and Kirstin, age three, dug out beach hats, towels, pails, and shovels. They set up their beach tent and towels on the floor and put on their bathing suits. They had a great time eating lunch and playing games at their pretend beach. Even ten-month-old Charles joined in the fun.

Party Favors

FILL A PLASTIC bucket with some of the day's necessities, including a shovel, sun visor, bottle of water, and snacks (shell candy, gummy fish, Goldfish crackers, and saltwater taffy), cheap sunglasses, and sunscreen.

Pail of Sand Cake

Family Olympics

THIS SUMMER COMPETITION, developed by *FamilyFun* contributor Jenifer Harms, pits family against family in a series of low-cost games the world-class event will never see. The event deserves a motto all its own. Forget "Faster, higher, stronger." These games are "Wackier, funnier, friendlier."

Opening Ceremony

SPARK THE OLYMPIC spirit with an official opening ceremony, where family teams carry a poster board pennant affixed to a broom and parade down the street to a taped rendition of the Olympic theme. After some inspirational words from the host, kids can race a foil and tissue paper torch across the playing field (a neighborhood or public lawn), and let the wacky games begin.

Olympic Torch

Olympic Torch: To make an official (albeit fake) torch, poke a hole in the center of the bottom of a plastic cup. Working from the center, make outward cuts like you would slice a pie. Next poke a hole in the center of a large yogurt lid and cut three "pie" slices. Now assemble the torch by slipping the lid up onto a paper towel tube, then slipping the cup down to meet the lid. Wrap foil around the entire torch and light it with tissue paper flames.

Winning Party Plans

When it comes to organizing games, the International Olympics Committee has nothing on Jenifer Harms. A mom and *FamilyFun* writer, she's been spearheading her neighborhood's Family Olympics for years. Here are her tips for making everything run like clockwork.

◆ **Choose your location early.** Jen held last year's games in a church gym. This year she'll move it outdoors and use traffic cones and ribbons as boundaries.

◆ **Use referees.** Jen recruits two grandparents and two college students to run the show.

◆ **Manage your time.** Jen hands each team an activity schedule on arrival and gives referees copies of the rules. She starts the games at 3 P.M. and ends them two hours later.

◆ **Pay attention to details.** The more authentic touches you can introduce into the events, the more memorable they will be. Give the referees whistles; hand out prizes; ask families to come in uniform.

◆ **Use a megaphone or a microphone.** It's the only way you'll be heard over the din.

◆ **Learn to love chaos.** Even good planning can't eliminate the craziness generated by a horde of kids.

Awards Ceremony

Olympic T-Shirts

Piggyback Parent

Tunnel Gopher

Family Olympics

Honorable Mentions

An Olympics without medals is like a birthday without cake. To make your own, write *first, second,* and *third* on plastic lids. Attach colored ribbons — blue for first, red for second, and white for third. Or, order real ribbons from a trophy store, such as Ribbon Ranch, Inc. (303-936-0231).

Mom-Calling Contest

IN THIS CONTEST, blindfolded mothers (or fathers) race to find their children, who are standing in a row and calling to them from a designated distance. Just imagine the roar of 50 kids bellowing all at once, "Mom, Mom, hey Mom!" (Crafty competitors have been known to cut through the clatter with a whistle, a move of debatable legality. Your Olympic committee will have to set its own guidelines.)

To get started, just line up all the parents and blindfold them. Next station the kids across an open expanse, making sure no obstacles come between them and their seeking parents. At a signal, the kids start screaming. The first parent-child team to make contact wins.

Mom-Calling Contest

Piggyback Parent

Piggyback Parent

IN THIS VARIATION on the 50-yard dash, parents have to carry their kids across the finish line. For single-child families, this will be a cinch. The dad who has to swing a seven-year-old on his back while wearing five-year-old twins on either hip faces a stiffer challenge.

As far as materials go, this event requires virtually nothing — just a start and a finish line. Competitors do need plenty of heart, however, since they can move forward only when their wee ones are completely off the ground. Here's one back-saving multichild strategy: shuttle the kids one at a time.

Tunnel Gopher

THIS RACE IS the opposite of leapfrog. Instead of jumping over the backs of teammates, players must tunnel through their legs toward the finish line.

Once again, all you need to get going is a start and a finish line. Begin by lining up families so they're facing the finish. At the start of the race, the last family member in line drops to the ground and crawls through the legs of everyone in front of him. Not until he stands up and spreads his feet can the next person at the end of the line begin. The team continues tunneling in this way until it reaches the finish line.

Free-Style Relay

Tunnel Gopher

Free-Style Relay

THIS RACE HAS as many legs as your largest family has members. Got a Brady Bunch among your friends? If so, each team must run eight legs. One more catch: Each leg consists of a different movement. For example, Leg 1: Cartwheels; Leg 2: Crab-walking; Leg 3: Skipping. Team members choose which lap or laps they want to run (it helps to keep track of the order on a sign board). The first family to finish a full round — one leg at a time — wins.

Olympic T-Shirts

To make your competition more realistic, have participating families create and wear their own uniforms. T-shirts can be printed, hand-painted, or simply color-coded.

Family Olympics

Shoe Pile Scramble

IN THIS GAME, children have to find their shoes and put them on. So what's the big deal? Don't we try to get them to do this at least once a day? Well, here the shoes of all the participating kids are scrambled in one big, sloppy heap.

To begin, players remove their shoes and pile them together. Mix everything up so no one pair is intact, then have the children stand side by side at the starting line. When the whistle blows, the kids race to find their shoes and fasten them before running back across the line. Children with siblings have to finish as a family.

Tug-of-War

A FAMILY-VERSUS-FAMILY tug-of-war is the crowning event of this contest, the marathon of the local Olympics.

A length of rope with a piece of tape marking the middle will get you started. Hint: The thicker the rope, the easier it is to hang on to and the less

Shoe Pile Scramble

likely it is to cause rope burns. To avoid injury, do not let contestants wrap rope around waists or wrists.

To begin, set two families at opposite ends of the rope and center the rope over a tape mark on the ground. Have the families step back 6 feet to another line marked with tape. At a signal, each family strains to pull the other across to its mark.

Run the contest like a tournament, picking family names out of a hat to determine who goes head-to-head in the first round. Winners keep advancing until only two families are left to square off for the championship.

Tug-of-War

Cake-Decorating Contest

Cake-Decorating Contest

T HIS EVENT MAKES the grade because it calls on creativity rather than athleticism. Plus it's always nice to have cake around.

Each family is allotted an identical premade, unfrosted, 9-inch, single-layer cake and a lump of white frosting. Participants also have access to a community supply of decorative frostings, berries, and candies, which they can use in whatever way they please.

Blow a whistle to start, then watch the frosting fly. Teams have 10 minutes to complete their works of art. The winner is decided by an open vote.

Jell-O Eating Contest

Jell-O Eating Contest

I N THE FINAL EVENT of the day, invite one member of each team to enter this silly, no-hands Jell-O Eating Contest. Prior to the party, prepare several packages of Jell-O as directed and bring them to the Olympic grounds in a cooler. Pack a measuring cup and several paper plates as well. Before the contest begins, the judge should put one cup of Jell-O per contestant on a plate and instruct each player to sit on his hands. When the judge calls "Go," players race to eat all the Jell-O. The first one to clean his plate wins a ribbon — and a full belly.

Awards Ceremony

A FTER EACH EVENT, winners stand atop cloth-draped milk crates to receive their medals (see Honorable Mentions on page 124). For an extra layer of authenticity, you can even play a tape recording of the familiar Olympic theme song. When the last medal has been awarded, tuckered out athletes traditionally tuck into a potluck supper — with prizewinning decorated cakes for dessert.

A Family Triathlon

For his tenth birthday, *FamilyFun* reader Kyle Campbell of Providence, Utah, planned a family triathlon. To prepare, he made a race number for each person, a finish line, and prizes. Contestants swam 25 laps in their backyard pool, raced mountain bikes up a rocky trail, and ran two laps around the block. Before crossing the finish line, they guzzled a can of soda. They celebrated with a backyard cookout.

Awards Ceremony

Fall Festival

APPLES, PUMPKINS, a lawn covered with leaves — when autumn is at its peak, there's no better time to round up the troops for a flurry of fun. Ask neighbors to bring their best apple pies to a bake-off, invite the kids to stuff a scarecrow, and for the grand finale, pile up all the leaves, and jump in and send them flying.

Fall Scavenger Hunt

Like squirrels, kids go nuts foraging for fall objects. Send the gatherers out with a list of things to find and a time limit. Depending on where you live, the list might include acorns, bark rubbings, berries, bird feathers, cattails, cocoons, cornstalks, birch or maple leaves, insects, milkweed pods, mushrooms, pinecones, river stones, seeds, and sticks. Remind young children not to eat anything they find — and to return living things to their natural habitats.

Autumn Atmosphere

YOUR BACKYARD will look a lot like an autumn party when you set out Indian corn, hay bales, and pumpkins on picnic tables or benches (have a display table for guests' own garden wonders, too). Welcome friends to your fall festival with signs that read "Fall Festival: Food, Games, and Fun." Tape the signs to sticks, push the sticks into a hay bale, and surround with a pile of leaves.

Hayrides

KICK THE PARTY off with a hayride through the backyard. Simply fill a wagon or riding mower trailer with hay. Then pull the kids around the yard and through the leaves. If a real hayride at a local orchard or farm is an option, reserve space for your group ahead of time. Ask guests to meet there before the party.

Leaf Pile Games

DON'T BAG UP those fallen leaves — instead, treat your guests to a round of leaf games. If you end up scattering the foliage even more during the festivities, don't despair. The final game, a leaf bagging contest, will leave your yard spotless.

Leaf Pile Hurdle: Arrange a row of leaf hurdles by raking up a series of small piles. Heap up a much bigger pile at the end of the row. One at a time, let the kids run and jump over the small piles and into the big one.

Leaf Labyrinth: When leaves cover the lawn, rake a classic maze path with rows and dead ends throughout. Then challenge the kids to find their way through the twisting paths.

Musical Piles: Make a circle of small leaf piles, one less than the num-

Leaf Pile Hurdle

ber of players. Follow the same rules used in musical chairs, playing a portable radio and raking away one pile each round.

Leaf-Blowing Contest: Ask each player to collect one large leaf, then assemble everyone side by side. Tell participants to tilt back their heads, hold their leaves just above their mouths, and puff heartily. The person whose leaf flies highest overhead wins.

Bag Them Up: Pair up players and place a supply of plastic lawn bags in a central spot. See which team can fill the most bags in a set amount of time.

Bob for Prize Apples

WHAT FUN WOULD a fall party be without bobbing for apples? Here's a variation on the basic rules of the game: Wash about ten apples and mark one with a special carving, or slice it deeply with a knife (a parent's job) and insert a foil-covered chocolate coin deep into the slit. Then set the apples in a big tub of water. To play, bobbers take turns trying to latch onto an apple with their teeth. The player who grabs onto the prize apple wins.

Pumpkin Painting

FOR A FALL art project that doubles as a party favor, let kids paint goofy, surprised, or creepy faces on pumpkins. Cover a picnic table with newspaper (tape it down so it doesn't blow away). Set out liquid tempera paints, paintbrushes, and plastic yogurt containers filled with water for rinsing the brushes, then paint away.

Scarecrow-Making Party

One way *FamilyFun* reader Patricia Vara of Gaithersburg, Maryland, celebrates the fall season is by getting friends together for a scarecrow-making party. She plans her party for early October when people are starting to think Halloween. Invitations instruct guests to B.Y.O.C. — Bring Your Old Clothes — for their scarecrow to wear. (The Varas supply the straw and head supplies.) Attire possibilities are endless: a tattered farm jacket, painter's overalls, a flashy suit and tie, flannel pajamas, an old Halloween costume, a secondhand prom dress, or an outgrown baseball uniform. Accessories, like a corsage, tiara, sunglasses, or a hat, add to the fun. Once all contestants have tucked the last bit of straw into their scarecrows, a warm potluck supper awaits them. The next day, scarecrows are proudly perched on front stoops — or standing on their heads — ready for Halloween.

Fall Food

KEEP THE FOOD simple — and familiar — at your party. You can provide hot dogs, fixings, and hot cider while guests bring side dishes or apple pies. Build a bonfire, pull up lawn chairs, and wait for the stars to come out.

Hot Dog Roast

When it's getting close to dinnertime, stoke the bonfire or prepare the coals for grilling. Set out hot dogs, buns, and all the fixings on a picnic table. Then guests can roast their own on the bonfire, or the designated parent can cook them on the grill.

Cinnamon Hot Cider

For the freshest taste, pick up gallons of pasteurized cider at a local orchard before the party. Serve it cold or hot in thermoses. To make spiced hot cider, pour 1 gallon of cider into a large saucepan. Tie 16 whole cloves, 10 allspice berries, and 2 sticks of cinnamon in a coffee filter and add to the cider. Cut 2 oranges into quarters and toss into the saucepan with the cider. Warm for 8 to 10 minutes over low heat. Serves 16.

Classic Apple Pie

No harvest celebration is complete without apple pies — and everyone claims his or her family's recipe is the

Caramel Apple Pie

Crowd Pleasers

best. So why not put it to the test? Cap the meal off with a pie tasting, then line the kids up for a no-hands pie-eating contest. Here's a recipe to get you started.

7 apples, peeled, cored, and sliced very thin (about 9 cups)

2 teaspoons cinnamon

3 tablespoons brown sugar

2 teaspoons all-purpose flour

1 unbaked piecrust (top and bottom)

In a large bowl, combine the apple slices, cinnamon, brown sugar, and flour. Line a 9-inch pie pan with piecrust, leaving a 1-inch overhang. Spoon in the filling. Roll out the remaining dough and set the whole crust (or lattice strips) on top of the fruit. Trim the edges, then fold the overhang under and crimp to seal the dough. Cut slits in the crust and add apple ornaments (made by cutting apples out of piecrust with cookie cutters). Preheat the oven to 400° and bake for 45 minutes, or until bubbly and golden brown.

Caramel Apple Pie: Follow the directions for the Classic Apple Pie, but make a lattice-top crust. While the baked pie cools, whip up a caramel sauce. In a small nonstick saucepan, melt 20 caramel candies with ¼ cup milk over low heat, stirring occasionally until smooth. Drizzle over the lattice-top pie, or cut individual slices of pie and pass the sauce.

Skating Party

PARTY STATS

Ages: All

Size: 10 to 20 guests

Length: 2 to 4 hours

Prep time: 2 hours

Cost: $1 per guest

GROWING UP IN New Hampshire, *FamilyFun* contributor Sam Mead would spend hours playing hockey on frozen Squam Lake with his brothers and sisters. Over the years, the gang perfected the outdoor skating party — a daylong event that includes plenty of friends, food, games, and, of course, a rinkside bonfire for warming numb toes.

Nice and Icy

YOU DON'T NEED to prepare for this party. Just wait for a day that's cold and crisp — and ice that's smooth and thick. Then make phone calls to invite friends, fill your thermoses with chicken soup and hot cocoa, and head to a local pond or lake. Clear a large area, lace up your skates, and let the games begin.

The Ice Train

THE PARTY officially begins when the Ice Train pulls out of the station. To form this conga line of skaters, just line up and grab the hips of the person in front of you, making sure to hold on tight. Of course, the lead person is the locomotive, so it's a good idea to position one of your stronger-skating adults at the head of the slithery line.

The Ice Train

Ice Skating Fun

SOMETIMES, the best games to play on the ice are the ones we're used to playing on dry land. Variations on tag are especially well suited to ice play.

Frozen Maze Tag: A layer of snow on the pond and a couple of shovels are all you need for this a-maze-ing game. To start, shovel lots of crisscrossing paths through the snow. When you've finished making your labyrinth, play the game like normal freeze tag. The only catch is that skaters have to remain within the cleared areas.

Skaters' Obstacle Course: Players get to show off all their moves in this game. To play, just set up an obstacle course by creating paths through boots, hockey sticks, sweaters, and any other items on hand. Try balancing sticks on top of boots for skaters to step or jump over. Or, two people can hold a stick at hip level that skaters pass under. To finish, all skaters must glide through a human tunnel, made by spectators.

Fox and Geese: Prepare for this game by shoveling a wagon-wheel shape in the snow, complete with hub and spokes. When you're ready to start, one player is designated the fox. His job is to chase the other players, the geese, in and around the wheel using the spokes (cleared paths) to cut across the circle. When the fox tags a goose, that person becomes a fox and joins in the hunt. The game is played until all the geese are caught. The last one to be tagged becomes the lead fox in the next game.

Skaters' Obstacle Course

Frosty Fashions

Partyers can step onto the ice in style by jazzing up their skates with pom-poms and beads. Offer them giant yarn pom-poms rinkside to tie onto their skate laces at the toes, or colorful pony beads (available at most craft stores) to string between the lace holes. The giant pom-poms make terrific party favors, too.

Skating Party

Quick Pick

To make teams, players toss their hats into a big heap. The hats are then randomly split into two equal piles — one for each side.

Hockey Play

A HOCKEY GAME often is the main event of a skating party. Before facing off, try warming up with these drills.

Monkey in the Middle: This icebreaker gives skaters a chance to practice their passing and puck control. Up to eight skaters form a big circle with one person standing in the center. The object is for the people around the circle to pass the puck without letting the monkey (in the middle) intercept it.

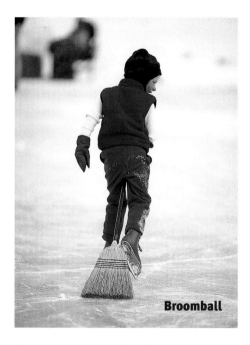

Broomball

Two safety rules: All sticks must be kept below the knees, and absolutely no flicking the puck in the air.

Sharpshooter: To test puck marksmanship, have all the players stand in the mouth of one hockey goal (formed by snow boots). One at a time, contestants take three long-distance shots on the goal at the opposite end of the rink. Having extra pucks helps keep the game moving.

Broomball

O NE OF THE BEST ways to introduce young skaters to the thrill of hockey is through broomball — in which young players use brooms and a rubber ball instead of sticks and a puck. A ball that's about the size of a bowling ball, or slightly smaller, and very light and bouncy makes the contest particularly fun. With a good wallop, players can send it ricocheting off knees and arms without worrying about anyone getting hurt. Set this game up like a hockey game, complete with snow boot goals (about 6 feet apart) and an equal number of players on each team (six is ideal). Start the game with a face-off at center ice.

Monkey in the Middle

Sled Race

Skating Races

ICE IS IDEAL for all kinds of sliding and towing races. These games are a great way to build skating muscles.

Sled Race: For this two-person team event, you'll need your blade sleds. One person sits on the sled while his partner pulls it over the ice. The object is to be the first team around the rink.

Backwards Hockey Pull: Another race (also good practice for skating backwards) is the hockey stick pull. Two team members face each other, holding the ends of two sticks between them. The puller skates backward, towing his partner along like a water-skier.

Ice Bowling

ON THE NIGHT before the party, fill ten (or more) clear plastic quart or liter bottles and several gallon jugs with water. Add a bit of food coloring to each, then put them out to freeze. To play, set out the quart containers as bowling pins, back up 10 feet or so, and use the frozen gallon jugs to topple the quarts.

Ice Bowling

Cold Feet?

Don't let numb toes slow you down. Warm your skates next to a woodstove or a heating vent before heading outside. Try a pair of silk socks instead of wool ones — the more room your toes have to breathe, the longer they stay warm.

Skating Party

Rinkside Dining

Triple-Axel Hot Chocolate

PROVIDING HEARTY nourishment off the ice is the secret to hosting a long, enjoyable party. And while a delicious cup of Triple-Axel Hot Chocolate (made with chocolate milk, chocolate chips, and cocoa powder) may warm a cold skater, it's more substantial foods like Chicken Soup with Rice that provide the energy to keep everyone's legs moving.

Because the bonfire will be used largely for warming hands and giving everyone a place to chat, set up a food table nearby and create the spread there.

Triple-Axel Hot Chocolate

A thermos of this hot cocoa, made with three kinds of chocolate, will give skaters an extra spin around the rink. For a double axel variation, you can omit the cocoa and sugar. Bring out Styrofoam cups and lots of mini marshmallows or whipped cream for serving the hot chocolate.

> ½ gallon milk
> ⅔ cup milk chocolate chips
> 6 tablespoons cocoa powder
> ⅓ cup sugar
> 1 quart chocolate milk
> Miniature marshmallows or
>   whipped cream (optional)

In a large saucepan over low heat, combine 1 cup of the milk with the chocolate chips, cocoa, and sugar. Whisk constantly until the mixture is smooth and the sugar is dissolved. Add the remaining milk and the chocolate milk and heat until steaming, but do not boil. Pour the drink into a preheated thermos, which will ensure that the drink stays hot. (To preheat a thermos,

Triple-Axel Hot Chocolate

136

fill with boiling water and let it sit for 5 minutes. Pour the water out, then fill with hot chocolate.) Before serving, shake the thermos to mix, pour into individual mugs, and top with marshmallows or whipped cream, if desired. Serves 12.

Chicken Soup with Rice

Before serving up this soup, challenge guests to recite Maurice Sendak's *Chicken Soup with Rice*. To refresh their memories, recite these lines: "In January / it's so nice / while slipping / on the sliding ice/to sip hot chicken soup / with rice. / Sipping once / sipping twice / sipping chicken soup / with rice."

    3 large carrots
    1 large onion, diced
    2 ribs celery, sliced ½ inch thick
    1 tablespoon vegetable oil
    10 cups low-sodium chicken broth
    1 cup converted long-grain rice
    3½ cups cooked chicken meat
        (1 pound uncooked), shredded or
        cut in 1-inch chunks
    2 tablespoons chopped parsley
    Salt and pepper to taste

Chicken Soup with Rice

Peel the carrots, slice into thin rounds, then cut into mini flowers using an aspic cookie cutter (or simply dice the carrots). In a large soup pot, sauté the carrots, onion, and celery in the oil over medium-high heat for 10

Sled Race

minutes, stirring occasionally. Add the chicken broth and rice, bring to a boil, then reduce the heat to low and simmer for 15 minutes. Add the chicken and continue cooking until the vegetables are tender, about 15 to 20 minutes. Add the chopped parsley, salt, and pepper and pour into a preheated wide-mouthed thermos (see directions under Triple-Axel Hot Chocolate). Serves 12.

Toasty the Snowman

This cute snowman on a stick can be roasted over the fire or eaten raw.

    3 marshmallows
    2 thin pretzel sticks
    Currants
    Apricots cut into small pieces
    Miniature M&M's
    Miniature chocolate chips

Roast all three marshmallows on one skewer until golden (a 2-foot-long green stick is the safest length for kids to use when cooking over a campfire). Carefully press the pretzel sticks, fruit, and chocolates into the toasted marshmallows for arms, eyes, a nose, and buttons.

Note: If you don't have a bonfire, just eat the decorated snowmen raw. If you have trouble getting the eyes and buttons to stay, snip small slits in the marshmallows, then insert the decorations. Serves 1.

Toasty the Snowman

Packing List for a Picnic on Ice

◆ Dry wood, kindling, newspaper, and waterproof matches for building a bonfire. (Be sure to get a permit and make the fire on the shore, not on the ice. Supervise carefully. For a safer alternative, bring a portable grill for warming food.)
◆ Blankets for seating
◆ A sled to use as a table, to transport food, and to carry tired skaters
◆ Styrofoam cups, plastic spoons, and napkins
◆ Tongs and oven mitts for working near the campfire
◆ Plastic bags for the garbage
◆ Plain hot water for tea and cleanups
◆ Extra mittens in case some get wet or lost

A Snow Ball

IN BIG SKY, MONTANA, where *FamilyFun* contributor Barbara Rowley lives, an average winter brings 33 feet of snow. With the drifts piling up one season, Barbara and family decided to quit fighting nature and just go with the flow. Thus was born the Snow Ball, a celebration of all things winter.

A Snowy Scene

UNLIKE MOST parties, a Snow Ball can't always be scheduled in advance. In most cases, all you can do is make preparations and then hope for a big snowstorm. While you wait, gather shovels, sleds, and snow clothes, stock up on supplies, and start eyeing the yard for good game sites. When the next blizzard strikes, you'll have this winter party plan down cold. Now all you have to do is call in the crowd.

The Iceman Smileth

AS THE OFFICIAL mascot of the Snow Ball, Frosty greets guests to the party. But this is a snowman with a difference — he's headless. This unique snowman is designed for great photo opportunities: kids stand behind the body and substitute their heads for the missing one — just like one of those cutouts found at carnivals. Place a small, sturdy stool behind the snow body so that shorter kids can get into the act, and make sure to have a few simple props at the ready, such as stocking caps and corncob pipes. If you have a Polaroid camera, the photos make fun take-home souvenirs. When everyone has had a turn mugging, roll a head for Frosty and complete it with the traditional carrot nose and coal button eyes. Now let the games begin.

A Snow Ball

A Snowball's Chance

KIDS CAN TOSS snowballs at trees, telephone poles, or each other any old winter day. The Snow Ball demands a more sophis-ticated test of marksmanship — a target traced in the snow. To make the bull's-eye, first stomp a flat circle about five feet across into the snow. Next use spray bottles filled with food coloring and water to draw concentric rings on the packed area. Make five rings in all, assigning each one a different point value — 5 (for the outermost ring), 10, 15, 20, and 25. To help players hone in on the target, make numbered flags that show the value of each section and plant them in the snow beside the rings. (Construction paper glued to craft dowels works nicely for the flags.) To play, give each contestant a bucket to fill with snowballs, then have them step back 15 feet to make their tosses. First player to reach 100 points wins. Don't be surprised if the game is cut short by a snowball war.

A Snowball's Chance

Ice Sculptures

In this art project, kids use blocks of colored ice to build fantastical sculptures. The night before the party, fill as many ice-cube trays, Jell-O molds, muffin tins, and yogurt cups with water as you can. Add a few drops of food coloring to each cup and set all the containers outside to freeze. (If you can spare the space, the ice will harden more consistently in the freezer.) When you're ready to begin building, place all the materials on an outdoor table. Dip the containers into warm water, and the ice blocks should slide out. Now everyone gets to pitch in and build totem poles, monsters, and sculptures — whatever imagination dictates. If the weather's cold enough, you can glue the blocks of ice with little dribbles of water — they should quickly freeze together.

An Angel for the Birds

MAKING SNOW ANGELS has a timeless appeal, but as a form of artistic expression it can be a little like stamping out cookies. To liven things up, try turning snow angels into festive mosaics. These colorful works of art, made with birdseed and pine boughs, will delight your feathered friends as much as they please your eye.

Have the kids work in teams: one partner flops down in the snow to make an angel imprint, while the other stands by to help the maker get up without stomping all over the image. Then, standing in each other's established foot holes, the snow artisans take turns pouring cups of birdseed into the angel, filling the head and body with bands of variously colored seed — thistle, corn, sunflower, and safflower work well together. (Younger kids may find it easier to fill their angels with just one type of birdseed.) Complete the mosaic by using pine boughs to make the angel's spreading wings.

An Angel for the Birds

A Snow Ball

It's a Dog's Race

It's a Dog's Race

THIS TOPSY-TURVY toboggan contest turns the tables on dogsledding, letting the dogs ride with the kids while the adults mush for the finish line. (The race needs to be short, since most dogs want to jump off their sleds almost immediately.)

The rules are simple: passengers have to hold the dogs on the sled; if Fido gets away, the riders must gather him up and return to the starting gate before proceeding. As it happens, a lot of the fun — at least for the humans — is in the dog-hugging, so nobody minds having to start over a few times.

If you don't have a dog, you can always substitute a pile of stuffed animals. Same rules apply.

Powder-Puff Football

A FRESH LAYER of snow can make for some slick moves and soft landings in this invigorating version of football. You'll need a football, two teams of three or more, and a spray bottle filled with water and food coloring to mark the playing field (a large rectangle with a centerline should suffice).

The teams line up at opposite ends of the field (the North and South Poles) for a kickoff. Once someone on the receiving team catches the football, he tries to move it back across the defense's goal line by running with it or passing it to a teammate. Play stops if the person with the ball is tagged by an opponent or slides out of bounds. The teams then face off again on the spot. After four tries, or a touchdown, the ball goes to the other team. The game ends when either team gets cold.

Frosty Food

FOR A WINTRY Buffet Table, use shovels to pile up, pack, and carve the snow into a table, then decorate the front with pine branches and cones. Set out thermoses of hot cocoa (see recipe on page 136), Styrofoam cups, and lots of mini marshmallows. For a seasonal surprise, offer ice cream made out of real snow.

Snow Ice Cream

In a blender, mix 1 pint whipping cream with ½ cup of sugar and 1 teaspoon vanilla extract for 3 minutes, or until thickened. Fill a large mixing bowl with clean snow. Pour the cream over the snow and stir well. Mix in chocolate syrup, fresh fruit, or crushed cookies, if desired, then dig in.

Après-Ski Fondue

When the party guests tire of playing in heaping piles of snow, invite them indoors to warm up with this quick and easy cheese fondue.

   1 10½-ounce can Cheddar cheese soup
1 cup grated Cheddar cheese
   Soft and hard breadsticks
   Apple and pear slices, celery sticks, and raw broccoli florets

Combine the soup and grated cheese in a microwave-safe bowl. Microwave on high for 2 minutes. Serve with the breadsticks, fruit, celery, and broccoli. Serves 8.

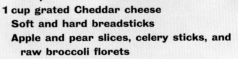

Crowd Pleasers

Backyard Cookout, page 147

Chapter Five

Dinner Parties

Backyard Cookout ★ Pizza Party ★ Italian Night
Super Salad Bar ★ Chinese Take-In
Mexican Fiesta ★ Potluck

IF THERE'S ONE thing that puts a group of people in a party mood, it's a home-cooked meal. The sight of bubbling Mozzarella on a homemade pizza, the sound of barbecued chicken sizzling on the grill, or the aroma of a fresh-baked apple pie can draw a crowd to the table in no time.

It's no surprise dinner parties are so popular with families. Besides providing a welcome reason to prepare and share our favorite dishes, a practice all too often forgotten in today's fast-paced world, dinner parties encourage our children to broaden their tastes — and their social graces. A sit-down meal with extended family or a group of friends is the perfect setting for kids and adults to slow down a little, swap-

ping stories and breaking bread.

The next time you host a dinner party, keep the following tips in mind. Not only will they help ensure the party's success, but they'll also save you time to spend with your guests.

Plan and prepare ahead: There's always something you can do a day or two in advance, such as crafting table decorations or chopping vegetables to store in plastic bags in the refrigerator until it's time to cook. And some casseroles and sauces actually taste better if you prepare them ahead of time.

Accept offers of help: If guests offer to bring something — whether it's dinner rolls, dessert, beverages, or even ice — let them. The contributions will afford you more time to focus on the main course.

Cheesy Nacho Appetizers, page 164

Dinner Parties

What About Manners?

They do matter, of course, but nothing splinters a party mood faster than overt nagging. Establish a set of subtle signals (with your kids' help) to serve as reminders for "Sit up straight," "Close your mouth," or "Elbows off the table."

Enlist the help of little hands: Setting the table for a dinner party can be done without having to dust off all your wedding crystal. Just relinquish your own ideas about what makes a table look perfect and turn some of the decorating tasks over to the kids. When they've contributed, they'll be more excited about the occasion. Kids who are artistically inclined will love making place cards or folding the napkins creatively. Any child can make a centerpiece, such as a prized LEGO creation, unshelled nuts arranged in a spiral, or even a shoe box diorama.

Create the mood: Lit candles have an almost magical effect on a room's ambience, especially if you are serving an evening meal. Even the youngest guests are fascinated by their glow, and the dimmer light has the added advantage of preventing everyone from seeing how dirty the tablecloth is getting!

Keep the youngest occupied: Very young kids simply can't sit still for longer than a few minutes, and there's no point in expecting them to. Let them bring a book or a small toy to the table. Remember, the point is to enjoy each other's company. If you have to resort to a few tricks (such as letting a youngster push a mini car around his plate or watching a plastic horse eat along with everyone else), who cares?

Plan conversation starters: Stockpile a few conversational topics (and subject-changers) in advance in case you need them. Icebreaker games like twenty questions or a few jokes and riddles are a good thing to have in reserve, too. And don't forget ideas for after-dinner entertainment, like a round of charades or a game of Monopoly.

Potluck Party, page 168

Backyard Cookout

WHETHER YOU USE A HIBACHI, a gas grill, or a charcoal-filled pit, a barbecue is a surefire way to a hungry dinner crew's heart. Besides bringing out the best flavors in meats and vegetables, it gets you out of the kitchen on a hot summer night and immediately creates an atmosphere of camaraderie and fun.

PARTY STATS

Ages: All
Size: 8 to 12 guests
Length: 2 to 3 hours
Prep time: 2 hours
Cost: $5 per guest

Before BBQing

THE KEY TO a successful cookout is patience — don't start cooking until the coals are red and glowing underneath and gray and ashy on top. There should be no discernible flames to char and dry out the food.

prepared grill. Use tongs to occasionally turn the dogs until they heat through and the skins are about to burst, about 5 to 8 minutes. Serve in toasted hot dog buns with mustard, relish, sauerkraut, or chili.

Great Grillables

Best-Ever Burgers

    2 pounds lean ground beef
    8 drops Worcestershire sauce
    1 teaspoon crushed oregano
      Salt and pepper to taste
    12 hamburger buns, split

Mix the beef, Worcestershire sauce, oregano, salt, and pepper, and form into 12 patties. When the coals are ready, place the burgers in the center of the grill and set the buns, opened and facedown, to the outside edge. As soon as the buns are toasted, flip the burgers and place a bun top on each. This will help the meat cook through. Serve with your favorite condiments.

Ultimate Hot Dogs

Choose hot dogs in their casings. Lightly score them and place on the

Ultimate Hot Dog

Dinner Parties

Backyard Cookout

Barbecued Chicken

1 large yellow onion, diced
2 tablespoons butter
2 large garlic cloves, minced
2 tablespoons water
¼ cup brown sugar
1 cup catsup
2 tablespoons white vinegar
1 tablespoon Dijon mustard
2 tablespoons Worcestershire sauce
1 teaspoon grated orange rind
¼ cup orange juice
4 chicken breasts
6 chicken legs or thighs

Sauté the onion in the butter, then add the garlic to the pan. When the onion becomes translucent, stir in the water and brown sugar and simmer for about 1 minute.

Add the catsup, vinegar, mustard, Worcestershire sauce, and orange rind, stirring all the while with a wooden spoon. Slowly pour the orange juice into the mixture and stir until blended. Continue to simmer over very low heat for 15 to 20 minutes, stirring occasionally. Set aside about ½ cup of the sauce for dipping, then brush the remaining amount on the chicken pieces several times while grilling. Serves 6 to 10.

Barbecued Chicken

Coat your grilled chicken (or even roasted corn and other vegetables) with this tangy, homemade sauce, and it won't take long for your dinner guests to follow their noses to the picnic table.

A Barbecue Buffet Table

There's nothing like a spread of picnic salads (see Super Salad Bar recipes, pages 156–159) and grilled vegetables and fruits to complement grilled burgers, dogs, and chicken. An easy option is to cook cherry tomatoes, onions, and peppers on metal skewers or barbecue corn on the cob. You can even grill fresh pineapple by placing thin slices on a rack over the hot coals and cooking them until lightly browned.

Whimsical Watermelon

Homemade Lemonade

AFTER CUTTING the lemons, you may want to turn this recipe over to the kids at your cookout — they tend to be the lemonade experts.

> 6 large lemons
> 1 cup sugar
> 2 quarts cold water

Slice the lemons in half and squeeze each of them into a large measuring cup. This should yield about 1½ cups of juice. Remove any seeds.

In a large pitcher or mason jar, combine the juice and the sugar. Stir in 2 quarts of cold water. Serve over ice. (For a nice touch, place mint leaves in the ice cube trays before freezing.) Serves 8 to 10.

Whimsical Watermelon

ANY WAY YOU slice it, a cookout just wouldn't be complete without a cool, juicy watermelon — and a seed-spitting contest.

By the Slice: Look for a melon that's symmetrical with no nicks or bruises. Then turn it over to make sure the underside is yellow (a sign of ripeness). Store at room temperature until you're ready to carve and serve it.

Seed-Spitting Contest: If you need advice on how to excel at this classic cookout competition, look to your kids, who are bound to be naturals. Declare contest winners for the highest, straightest, most comical, and farthest spit. For ground rules, follow the advice of the National Watermelon Association: no blowing tubes and no running, skipping, or lying down.

Cookout Games

AFTER YOUR GUESTS have had their fill (and a little time to digest), cap off your cookout with a game of croquet or horseshoes.

Horseshoes

Decorate a Tablecloth

When *FamilyFun* reader Amanda Walker of Camden, Alabama, hosts a cookout, she covers her tables with plain newsprint and sets crayons at each place setting. As families arrive, they can decorate their places on the tablecloth. Or, take advice from *FamilyFun* reader Denise Radecke of Cordova, Tennessee, and let guests personalize plastic cups with markers and glitter pens.

Pizza Party

IF THERE'S ONE FOOD that's a natural crowd pleaser, it's pizza. And while it's a cinch to have one delivered, this deprives your kids and their friends of half the fun: rolling up their sleeves and turning dough, sauce, and cheese into their very own pizza pies. With a bit of preparation, this party can be a rewarding way to both entertain and feed young guests.

Pizza Party Prep

WHETHER YOUR KIDS opt to phone in their pizza party invitations or send written ones through the mail (you can cut pizza slice–shaped invitations out of colored paper), ask the guests to bring their own aprons or, at least, to wear clothes they can cook in. On the party day, spread a plastic-coated tablecloth on the table and supply paper plates and plenty of paper napkins. There's no need for utensils: the kids can use their fingers — for cooking and eating.

Time to Make the Pizzas

Quick Dough

This recipe makes enough for two 12-inch pizzas or eight small ones and only takes about 15 minutes to rise. (To double the recipe, remember that the ratio is 3 parts flour to 1 part liquid.) You can save time during the party by making the dough in advance and storing the unrisen rolled-out rounds (stacked between sheets of waxed paper) in the freezer for up to a month.

> 1 package active dry yeast
> 1 cup lukewarm water
> 1 tablespoon sugar
> 1 teaspoon salt
> 3 cups all-purpose flour, sifted
>   Additional flour or cornmeal for
>   rolling out the dough

Dissolve the yeast in water in a food processor or mixing bowl and let stand for 5 minutes. Stir in the sugar and salt. Mix in 1½ cups of flour. Add the rest of the flour, processing or stirring until the dough forms a ball. Turn out the dough onto a board dusted with flour or cornmeal and knead for about 5 minutes until the dough is smooth.

Pizza Party

150

Divide it into equal round portions and roll and gently stretch out. Press onto pans, cover with a dry towel, and let rise in a warm, draft-free place for 15 minutes. The crusts are then ready for toppings.

Pizza Toppers

In separate bowls, set out 2 cups of plain tomato sauce, 3 cups of grated Mozzarella cheese sprinkled with 1 tablespoon of olive oil, 4 sliced carrots, 1 cup of sliced fresh mushrooms, 1 cup of sliced zucchini, 1 cup of blanched broccoli florets, 1 cup of chopped cooked spinach, ½ pound of sliced pepperoni, 1 diced green or red pepper, 1 cup of grated Parmesan cheese, and ½ cup of chopped black olives. Now the kids can pick and choose ingredients to arrange

Pizza Toppers

on their pies, creating funny faces or even a landscape. When the pizzas are assembled, place them in a preheated 450° oven for 10 to 15 minutes, or until the cheese is melted and the bottoms of the crusts are golden. Then slice them up (a parent's job) and enjoy.

Pizza Funny Faces

A Restaurant-Style Party

According to *Family Fun* reader Zee Ann Poerio from Bethel Park, Pennsylvania, her kids especially look forward to their family's restaurant-style supper parties. For a menu, Zee Ann prints the dinner courses on a piece of paper, and the kids decorate it with crayons or markers. Then everyone takes turns being a host, a busboy, or a waiter (even young kids can scribble an order the "chef" will be able to read). And there's a reward for service with a smile — a modest tip!

151

Italian Night

PARTY STATS

Ages: All
Size: 8 to 10 guests
Length: 2 to 3 hours
Prep time: 3 hours
Cost: $5 per guest

YOU DON'T HAVE TO COME from the old country to pull off an Italian dinner party for family and friends. Just put on some Italian pop music or an opera, pour grape juice for a festive *salute!*, and serve a hearty pasta dish to swirl and slurp. Then cap off the evening with biscotti and an Italian game.

An Italian Tabletop

ALL IT TAKES to dress your table Italian style is a checked tablecloth, candles, and cloth napkins for guests to tuck into their shirts before digging in. And don't forget a basket of breadsticks.

Tomatoes with Mozzarella

An Italian Feast

Tomatoes with Mozzarella

Once the guests have been seated, bring on this tasty tomato appetizer. It's made with balls of fresh Mozzarella, which you can find packaged with water or whey at most grocery stores.

6 tablespoons fresh basil leaves, torn
1 pound fresh ciliegine Mozzarella
   (cut into bite-size pieces)
   Pinch of dried oregano
   Pinch of salt
1 teaspoon freshly ground pepper
½ cup extra-virgin olive oil
1 pound cherry tomatoes, cut in half

Combine the basil, Mozzarella, oregano, salt, and pepper in the olive oil and marinate for 1 hour at room temperature. Just before serving, toss in the tomatoes. Serves 8 to 10.

Spaghetti with Meatballs and Sauce

MEATBALLS:
1½ pounds ground beef
½ pound ground sweet
   or hot Italian sausage
6 tablespoons grated Parmesan
   cheese

Italian Night

Pasta Doodles

If you end up with any leftover spaghetti, offer your young guests a bowlful to turn into instant art. Just set out a few sheets of construction paper and let everyone stick on the cooked noodles, shaping them into flowers,

faces, or scenic landscapes. If a child wants to take a favorite drawing home, cover it with waxed paper and top with a heavy book so that it will dry flat.

Spaghetti with Meatballs and Sauce

¼ cup bread crumbs
¼ cup finely chopped onion
1 teaspoon dried basil
1 teaspoon salt
4 garlic cloves, minced
2 eggs
4 to 6 tablespoons olive oil

TOMATO SAUCE:

2 medium onions, finely chopped
6 tablespoons finely grated carrot
3 tablespoons olive oil
4 garlic cloves, minced
2 28-ounce cans crushed tomatoes
  Salt to taste

2 pounds of spaghetti
  Grated Parmesan cheese

To make the meatballs, mix all the ingredients except the olive oil and form into 1-inch balls (the size of small walnuts). In a large sauté pan, brown the meatballs in the oil until cooked through, about 8 to 10 minutes. Drain on paper towels.

To make the tomato sauce, sauté the onion and carrot in the olive oil for 3 to 4 minutes over medium-high heat. Add the garlic and cook for another minute.

Toss in the tomatoes and reduce the heat to medium. Cook another 10 to 15 minutes. Add salt to taste, then the meatballs.

While the meatballs simmer in the sauce, bring a pot of water to a boil. Add a tablespoon of cooking oil to the water (this will keep the noodles from sticking together while they cook). Stir in 2 pounds of pasta and cook it al dente, or slightly chewy. Fill individual bowls with the cooked pasta and top with meatballs, sauce, and grated Parmesan cheese. Serves 8 to 10 (makes about 4 to 5 dozen meatballs and 6 cups of sauce).

Green Salad

Italian tradition calls for serving salad at the end of the meal. For an authentic *insalata*, fill individual salad bowls with greens — iceberg, romaine, and chicory. At the table, let each person sprinkle the greens with salt, olive oil, and a splash of wine vinegar or lemon juice (about 3 parts oil to 1 part vinegar or lemon juice). Toss the greens and enjoy.

Biscotti

These crunchy, twice-baked cookies are just right for dipping in milk, hot cocoa, or coffee, or serving with that everyday Italian dessert — fresh fruit.

    ¾ cup chopped almonds
    ½ cup unsalted butter, softened
    ¾ cup sugar
    3 eggs
    1 tablespoon vanilla extract
    3 ounces semisweet chocolate, melted
        and cooled
    ⅓ cup cocoa
    1½ teaspoons baking powder
    ¼ teaspoon salt
    2 cups all-purpose flour

In an oven preheated to 325°, toast the almonds until light brown, shaking the pan occasionally. Let cool. Cream the butter and sugar until fluffy. Beat in the eggs, vanilla extract, and melted chocolate. Mix in the cocoa, baking powder, salt, flour, and almonds (the dough will be very soft).

Shape the dough into two 14- by 3- by ½-inch logs. Place each log on a waxed-paper-lined baking sheet and cover loosely with plastic wrap. Freeze for 1½ to 2½ hours. Remove the plastic wrap and bake in an oven preheated to 325° for 30 to 35 minutes.

Remove the logs and cool for 5 minutes. With a serrated knife and a firm stroke (to minimize the crumbling), slice each log diagonally into ½-inch pieces. Lay the biscotti cut side down on the baking sheet and bake for another 6 to 8 minutes. Flip to the other side and bake 6 to 8 minutes more, or until the cookies turn a light chocolate brown, but not too dark. Cool completely on a wire rack. Makes about 3 dozen.

Play Bocce

After dinner, team up for a popular Italian pastime — a round of bocce. If you don't have a set of bocce balls, try your luck at an early version of the game, played in the Italian Alps about 2,000 years ago. Place a stone or another small object in the center of the backyard and then take turns tossing pebbles, or pennies, at it. Whoever lands his or her pebble or coin closest to the stone wins.

Green Salad

Super Salad Bar

PARTY STATS

Ages: All

Size: 8 to 12 guests

Length: 2 to 3 hours

Prep time: 3 hours

Cost: $5 per guest

IF YOU'RE LOOKING for a fun, casual party meal for a crowd, it's hard to beat a salad bar, especially in summer when produce is at its peak. It's as simple as this: fill serving dishes with greens, chopped raw vegetables, and a few side-dish salads, and line them up on a table. Guests get to choose the foods they like, and you get to relax and enjoy, knowing there'll be plenty for everybody — even the pickiest eaters.

Set Up a Buffet

FOR THE BEST results, place dinner plates, utensils, and napkins at one end of the buffet table and the salad fixings, bread, and butter at the other. For side dishes that need to be kept cold, set the serving bowls in ice-filled containers. Add a bouquet of fresh herbs, such as basil, parsley, cilantro, or dill, to snip into small pieces on request. Then set up a smaller table for condiments and beverages.

Salad Bar Buffet

Side Dishes

IN ADDITION to the classic salad bar staples (see The Making of a Great Salad Bar below), set out the following side dishes, some of which can be prepared ahead of time.

Tingly Fruit Salad

Prepare this berry and melon combination a few hours before the party, and it will develop a light, sweet syrup.

> 1 pint raspberries
> 1 pint blueberries
> 1 small honeydew melon
> 1 small cantaloupe
> 2 teaspoons sugar
> ½ cup fresh mint leaves
>   (optional)

Rinse the berries and let dry. Seed and cube the melons. In a stainless steel or glass bowl, toss together the fruit and sugar. Cover and chill for 3 hours.

Right before serving, wash the mint. Use scissors to snip it into small pieces. Toss in with the fruit. Serves 8.

Chicken Salad Fiesta

Salsa gives this salad an unexpected kick. If you don't have leftover chicken, you can buy roasted chicken at the deli or cook 1½ pounds of boned, skinless chicken breast.

> 1 small garlic clove,
>   minced
> 1 tablespoon olive oil
> 1 tablespoon lemon juice
> ¾ cup salsa
>   Salt and pepper to taste
> ½ cup finely diced red bell
>   pepper

Tingly Fruit Salad

The Making of a Great Salad Bar

To be sure your guests have a well-balanced choice of ingredients for fixing their dinner salads, include a few items from each of the following categories on your buffet table.

Greens: Romaine or iceberg lettuce, mesclun, spinach, or Swiss chard (these will hold up longer than leaf lettuce).

Vegetable Toppings: Strips of green, red, or yellow bell peppers, edible pea pods, shredded red cabbage, broccoli or cauliflower florets, sliced cucumbers, cherry tomatoes, or carrot sticks.

Protein Add-Ins: Grated cheese, smoked turkey or ham cubes, crumbled bacon, salami strips, or chickpeas.

Spoon-Ons: Chopped peanuts, croutons, pitted olives, raisins, or sunflower, pumpkin, or sesame seeds.

Salad Dressing: For a variety of tastes, set out two or three different dressings, such as a vinaigrette, blue cheese, and ranch.

Super Salad Bar

Kernels from 2 ears of cooked corn, or
1 cup frozen corn kernels, thawed
⅔ cup small pitted ripe black olives
4 cups cooked chicken, diced

In a bowl, combine the garlic, olive oil, lemon juice, salsa, salt, and pepper. Stir in the remaining ingredients. Cover and chill for up to 3 days. Serves 6 to 8.

New Potato Salad

This picnic favorite gets its creamy texture not from mayonnaise, but from its mustard vinaigrette dressing.

4 pounds new potatoes, unpeeled
6 tablespoons cider vinegar
4 tablespoons canned
  chicken broth
½ cup vegetable oil
3 tablespoons Dijon mustard
¼ cup minced onion
4 hard-boiled eggs, finely chopped
4 stalks celery, finely chopped
2 teaspoons salt
  Black pepper to taste

Boil the potatoes in a large pot of water for about 30 minutes, or until tender. Do not overcook. Drain and set aside for about 20 minutes. In a large bowl, combine the remaining ingredients.

Slice the warm potatoes and toss with the dressing mixture until well coated. Cover and let set for 1 hour. Refrigerate for up to 2 days. Serves 8.

Corkscrew and Tomato Salad

This dish is best prepared right before the party and served at room temperature. The corkscrew pasta is ideal for trapping the tasty dressing. Just be sure to rinse the cooked pasta under cold running water before adding the other

New Potato Salad

Corkscrew and Tomato Salad

ingredients, or it will continue to cook in the oil and vinegar and turn mushy.

> 1 pound corkscrew pasta
> ½ cup olive oil
> ¼ cup balsamic vinegar
> 1 small garlic clove, peeled
> ½ cup walnuts
> 1 teaspoon salt
>   Fresh pepper to taste
> 4 medium tomatoes
> 1 can (16 ounces) white beans,
>   drained and rinsed

Cook the pasta al dente in 4 quarts of boiling salted water. Drain, then cool the pasta under running water.

In a blender or food processor, puree the olive oil, balsamic vinegar, garlic, and walnuts until smooth. Season with salt and pepper.

Dinner Parties

Halve the tomatoes, remove the seeds, and chop into bits. Mix with the beans and dressing in a bowl. Pat dry the pasta and add it to the other ingredients. Marinate for 30 minutes. Serves 8.

Salad Party: Take Two

There's no need for salad bar leftovers to go to waste. All those cut-up vegetables can be the beginning of one of the following nutritious meals just right to serve at a lunch or supper party with a few family friends.

Vegetable Soup
Simmer mixed chopped vegetables in chicken or beef broth until tender. Add grated cheese right before serving.

Garden-Style Pasta
Sauté cut-up vegetables in olive oil until tender. Add cubes of ham or turkey. Stir in tomato sauce and serve over pasta with grated cheese.

Stir-Fry Supper
Cook leftover vegetables in peanut oil just until tender. Stir in cubes of turkey or ham and ladle over rice. Spoon on sesame seeds or chopped peanuts.

Chinese Take-In

WHETHER YOU'RE DIPPING dumplings or filling and folding Moo Shu pancakes, there's something about eating Chinese that instantly puts you in a party mood. But before you order takeout, check out the following plan for whipping up a Chinese feast in your own kitchen. It's easier than you think, and twice the fun.

Chopsticks

Providing chopsticks (sold at Asian grocery stores) is a fun way to give your Chinese dinner party an authentic touch. For guests who have never used them, fold a business card accordion style and put it between a pair of chopsticks near the tops. Wrap a rubber band in a figure eight around the sticks and over the card. Now the sticks will work like tweezers.

Set the Table for Chinese Take-In

A CENTERPIECE AS simple as a flowering branch set in a glass vase and a lucky red tablecloth can add a traditional flair to your dinner table. Don't forget a pot of hot tea and small bowls of soy sauce, duck sauce, and mustard.

A Chinese Menu

Steamed Dumplings

These delectable meat-filled dumplings, served with small bowls of dipping sauce (¼ cup soy sauce mixed with 2 tablespoons white vinegar), make a great appetizer for your Chinese dinner party.

3 stalks Chinese cabbage
2 scallions
1 tablespoon soy sauce

Chopsticks

Steamed Dumplings

1 teaspoon salt
1 tablespoon cornstarch
1 pound lean ground pork
1 10-ounce package prepared dumpling wrappers (available at Asian food stores)

Finely chop the Chinese cabbage and scallions and put them in a mixing bowl. Add the soy sauce, salt, cornstarch, and pork. Mix well with a spoon.

Place 1 teaspoon of filling on each wrapper. Fold the wrappers into half circles. Moisten the inside edges with water and press them together to seal.

In a large pot, bring 2 quarts of water to a boil. Drop in the dumplings and cover. When the water resumes boiling, add 1 cup cold water. Repeat this step twice. When the water boils for the third time, the dumplings will be done. Makes 4 dozen.

Moo Shu Pork

Chinese Take-In

Dinner from Other Lands

FamilyFun reader Patty Rawlison, from Riverside, California, got one of her family's favorite dinner party ideas while she was on a cruise: international cuisine. Every Sunday, the family meal is inspired by a different country.

While dining on an authentic menu, they try to use at least a few words spoken in the native language. And they make a point of discussing the customs of that land. After dinner, they draw an outline of the country's flag for the kids to color and post on the refrigerator door.

Sesame Noodles

Sesame Noodles

The kids at your dinner party will love the taste of these nutty noodles.

> 1 tablespoon tahini (sesame paste)
> 1 cup smooth or chunky unsweetened peanut butter
> 2¼ tablespoons white vinegar or rice vinegar
> 1½ cups chicken stock
> 1½ teaspoons powdered ginger
> 1 tablespoon soy sauce
> ¾ pound spaghetti, or Chinese egg noodles, cooked al dente
> 3 tablespoons peanut oil
> 3 whole scallions, sliced crosswise
> 1½ cups mung or soybean sprouts, rinsed and drained (optional)

In a small bowl, combine the tahini, peanut butter, vinegar, stock, ginger, and soy sauce. Toss the noodles with peanut oil just to coat. Toss with the tahini sauce, then chill. Just before serving, garnish with scallions and bean sprouts. Serves 8 to 10.

Moo Shu Pork

For authentic Moo Shu, you need "tree ears" (Chinese black mushrooms), bean thread noodles, and mandarin pancakes. This recipe uses foods that are easier to find, without sacrificing taste.

FILLING:

> 2 tablespoons soy sauce
> 1 tablespoon dry sherry
> 1 tablespoon cornstarch
> ¾ teaspoon sugar
> 2¼ pounds pork tenderloin, trimmed and cut into strips ¼ inch thick
> 6 tablespoons peanut oil
> 1½ cups mung or soybean sprouts, rinsed and drained
> 12 scallions, cut in half and julienned

Chinese Lanterns

PANCAKES:

18 mandarin pancakes (available at Chinese grocery stores) or 18 large flour tortillas

SAUCE:

6 tablespoons hoisin sauce
2 tablespoons dry sherry
2 tablespoons soy sauce
1½ tablespoons sugar

To make the filling, stir together the soy sauce, sherry, cornstarch, and sugar. Marinate the pork in the mixture while you prepare the pancakes and sauce.

Wrap the pancakes or tortillas in foil and warm for 10 minutes in a 325° oven. In a small bowl, mix together the ingredients for the sauce.

Heat the peanut oil in a frying pan over high heat. Add the pork strips and stir-fry for 3 minutes, or until the meat is no longer pink. Restir your hoisin mixture and add it to the pan, tossing the pork for a few seconds to coat it evenly. Stir in the bean sprouts, then remove the combination to a serving platter and top with the scallions.

To serve, spoon the stir-fry into the center of a pancake, fold up one inch at the bottom, then fold over the sides and eat with your hands. Serves 8 to 10.

Dessert Chinese Style

When everyone's had enough Moo Shu, bring on dessert: ginger ice cream served with mandarin oranges and store-bought fortune cookies.

Chinese Lanterns

For a party decoration, make colorful Chinese Lanterns. For each one, fold an 8½- by 11-inch sheet of paper in half lengthwise. Cut 3½-inch slits into the fold and parallel to the short edges. Start an inch from each edge and leave a half inch between slits. Unfold the paper and glue the short edges together. Glue a paper handle to the lantern and hang.

Rock, Paper, Scissors

For a little after-dinner entertainment, invite the younger party guests to try their luck at a classic game of rock, paper, scissors played the way kids do in China. Here's how:

Two kids sit side by side at the bottom of a short staircase. On the count of three, both of them must throw one hand forward in the form of a rock (a fist), paper (fingers held together straight out), or scissors (forefinger and middle finger in a V). Following the logic that paper covers rock, rock breaks scissors, and scissors cut paper, the player who presents the winning symbol in that round moves up one step. If both

kids display the same symbol, it's considered a tie. Play continues in this manner until one child reaches the top step and wins the game.

Mexican Fiesta

A S HER FAMILY'S chief party planner, *FamilyFun* contributor Rebecca Okrent relies heavily on Mexican fare, especially when a gang of hungry kids is threatening like rain clouds. She prepares fillings for tacos, tostadas, or burritos, mixes an ice-cold pitcher of kids' sangria, hangs a piñata — and it's an instant fiesta!

A Mexican Buffet

One of the best things about eating Mexican is deciding which toppings and fillings to load up your tortilla with. For the ultimate spread of choices, set out bowls of refried beans, spicy beef filling, shredded cheese, shredded lettuce, chopped tomatoes, diced bell peppers, sliced black olives, salsa, guacamole, sour cream, and minced jalapeños.

Mexican Mood Setters

F OR A DISTINCTIVE south-of-the-border flair, start with Mexican music (you may be able to track down tapes by Flaco Jimenez, La Tropa F, Texas Tornadoes, or Los Lobos at your local library). You can also hang bright-colored streamers and replace your ordinary lightbulbs with green, blue, red, and yellow ones.

The Menu

Cheesy Nacho Appetizers

1-pound bag of tortilla chips
12-ounce can of refried beans
½ pound grated Monterey Jack or mild Cheddar cheese
Salsa Fresca
(see recipe at right)

Preheat the oven to 375°. Spread the chips on a baking tray and spoon on the refried beans. Top with the grated cheese.

A Mexican Buffet

Cheesy Nacho Appetizers

Once a month, the Muros, *FamilyFun* readers in Sparks, Nevada, add sparkle to their supper hour by planning a themed dinner. Everyone wears appropriate attire and brings fun facts, music, or activities to share or perform following the meal. For their debut, they dined Asian style, wearing robes and using chopsticks; during their country-and-western meal they played music from Garth Brooks and read cowboy poetry; and for their Dr. Seuss meal, they feasted on a colorful menu inspired by *Green Eggs and Ham*.

Bake until the cheese just melts (about 4 minutes). Serve with salsa. Serves 8.

Salsa Fresca

Also known as *pico de gallo*, this salsa is made with fresh cilantro — a flavor that makes any dish taste Mexican.

    2 garlic cloves
    1 jalapeño peppers, sliced in half,
        seeded, and deveined
    1 medium onion, quartered, or
        1 bunch scallions, chopped
    ¼ cup cilantro leaves
    2 large tomatoes (or 6 small ones),
        cored and quartered

In the bowl of a food processor, chop the ingredients in the order listed above. Drop each ingredient into the processor with the blades running, turning the machine off between additions (avoid liquefying the tomatoes). Spoon leftover sauce into a jar, pour a tablespoon of vegetable oil over the top, and refrigerate. Makes 3 cups.

Spicy Beef Tacos or Tostadas

Both of these Mexican sandwiches begin with crispy corn tortilla shells — folded for tacos or open-faced for tostadas. You can buy a box of either kind in the international section of your grocery store. Heat them briefly (according to the package directions). Then spoon on spicy beef filling, and let guests top off their shells with shredded lettuce, grated cheese, chopped tomatoes, sliced olives, salsa, or sour cream.

Mexican Fiesta

Fold Your Own Burrito

The same toppings that taste great on tacos or tostadas are perfect for filling burritos. Just wrap a stack of soft flour tortillas in foil and bake in a preheated 400° oven for about 3 minutes. Guests can spoon fillings onto the warm tortillas and fold their own burritos (beginning with the sides, then the top, and finally the bottom of the tortilla, as shown).

Spicy Beef Tostadas

1 tablespoon vegetable oil
1 cup chopped onion
2 pounds lean ground beef
4 garlic cloves, crushed
⅔ cup tomato juice or beef stock
4 tablespoons chili powder
1 teaspoon cumin
Salt and pepper to taste

Heat the oil in a skillet over medium heat. Add the onion and sauté until soft. Break up the ground beef with a fork and add it to the skillet. Add the garlic and continue stirring until the meat browns, then drain any excess fat. Stir in the tomato juice or beef stock, chili powder, cumin, and salt and pepper. Continue cooking, stirring occasionally, until the mixture is heated through. Makes 4 cups.

Mexican Rice

To cut preparation time for this recipe, use a food processor to chop the onions, garlic, and pepper.

1 tablespoon vegetable oil
1½ cups white rice, uncooked
1 16-ounce can Italian plum tomatoes, peeled and chopped, with their juice
2 medium onions, chopped
2 garlic cloves, crushed
1 jalapeño pepper, seeded, deveined, and chopped
½ teaspoon cumin
2 cups chicken stock, tomato juice, or water
1 cup frozen corn kernels
Fresh parsley or cilantro (optional)

Heat the vegetable oil in a large saucepan and add the rice. Stir until it has turned white, about 3 minutes. Add the tomatoes, onion, garlic, pepper, cumin, liquid, and corn. Bring to a boil, then simmer, covered, until the liquid is absorbed and the rice is tender, about 15 minutes. Garnish with chopped fresh parsley or cilantro. Serves 8.

Kids' Sangria

2 quarts cranberry/raspberry juice
6 oranges, thinly sliced
4 limes, thinly sliced

In a large pitcher, stir the juice and fruit. Pour into ice-filled glasses. Serves 10.

Flan

For a traditional sign-off to your Mexican menu, serve this sweet, smooth custard bathed in caramel syrup.

TOPPING:

2 tablespoons water
½ teaspoon vanilla extract
½ cup sugar

FILLING:

3 eggs
3 egg yolks
¾ cup sugar
13½ ounces evaporated milk
1 cup whole milk
1 teaspoon vanilla extract

Heat the water, vanilla extract, and ½ cup of sugar in a heavy skillet, stirring until the mixture comes to a boil. Use a wet pastry brush to brush down sugar crystals from the pan's sides. Allow the syrup to boil undisturbed until it is a rich amber color. Immediately remove the pan from the heat. Scrape the caramel into a 9-inch round cake pan, moving the pan to coat the bottom and sides.

For the filling, beat the eggs and yolks in a bowl. Add the sugar, then beat for 1 minute. Beat in the remaining ingredients. Pour into the cake pan and cover with foil. Set the pan in a larger baking pan filled halfway with water. Bake at 350° for 1 hour, or until set. Cool for 30 minutes, then refrigerate. To serve, run a knife around the rim of the custard and invert it onto a serving dish. Serves 8.

Break a Piñata

To make sure your fiesta is a smashing success, hang a piñata. The youngsters in your dinner crowd will love the chance to be blindfolded, hit something really hard (with a broomstick or bat), and, of course, win prizes. You can buy a piñata at a party store or make your own (see page 17). Mark off a striking area with crepe paper (to keep partygoers away from the stick-wielding kid) and tell the kids that whatever prizes they pick up when it breaks will be collected in a bag, then divided.

Flan

Potluck Party

WHEN YOU'RE ENTERTAINING a crowd, a potluck has some built-in advantages. With a little planning, time-strapped parents get to see their friends without having to cook a full-course meal. Kids can try small samples of all the entrées and desserts. And cleanup is easy because everyone takes home their own dishes.

Invitations

FOR INEXPENSIVE invitations that the whole family can help out with, start with a photo of a past potluck party. Have it photocopied onto sheets of paper along with all the party particulars. At home, your kids can hand-color the invites. Add a

Potluck Invitation

Please come to the Smiths' house...

The Buffet Table

personal note to each, asking a certain number of guests to bring beverages, salads, main dishes, or desserts and to R.S.V.P. Then fold, tape, and address the invitations, and they're ready to mail.

The Buffet Table

O NCE YOU KNOW how many guests plan to attend and what dishes they'll bring, prepare a self-serve buffet area. A long table or counter is ideal. At one end, stack dishes, cutlery, and napkins. Reserve the adjacent area for salads and other cold dishes and arrange a bunch of trivets at the far end for hot dishes, which can be kept warm in the oven until the last minute. Set up a separate card table for condiments, beverages, an ice bucket, and desserts.

Great Potluck Picks

M OST FAMILIES probably will have a favorite dish they'll want to contribute. If not, suggest that they bring a recipe that begins with the letter of their name, such as Laura's lemon cake or the Smiths' scalloped potatoes. Or ask

Fruit Kabob Critter

Dinner Parties

Spaghetti Pie

them to bring one of the following tried-and-true potluck classics.

Fruit Kabob Critter

    1 seedless watermelon
    2 cantaloupes
    2 honeydew melons
      Wooden skewers

Cut the melons in half lengthwise and use a melon baller to scoop out melon balls. Push the melon balls onto skewers. For a fun presentation, turn the kabobs into a fruity porcupine by sticking the bottoms of the skewers into an inverted scooped-out watermelon half. You can even attach other fruits to create a face. Serves 12 to 20.

A Recipe Swap

When *FamilyFun* reader Mandy McMillen of Spencer, Tennessee, attends a potluck dinner, she slips extra copies of her recipe into a sealable plastic bag and places it near her dish at the serving table.

A Giant Grinder

Come In from the Cold

In Hotchkiss, Colorado, *FamilyFun* reader Vicki Hodges hosts a cozy soup potluck every winter. Her friends bring soup in a crock pot and crackers or biscuits to share.

Spaghetti Pie

Olive oil
2 cups cooked spaghetti
1½ cups tomato sauce
2 teaspoons dried basil
½ cup grated Parmesan cheese
½ cup grated Monterey Jack
or Mozzarella cheese
¼ cup sliced black olives

Preheat the oven to 350°. Brush a 9-inch pie pan with a little olive oil. In a large mixing bowl, stir together the spaghetti, tomato sauce, basil, and grated Parmesan cheese. Spread the spaghetti into the oiled pie pan. Sprinkle the Monterey Jack or Mozzarella cheese on top and garnish with the olives. Bake for 20 to 30 minutes, or until the pie turns brown and crispy on top. Slice and serve. Makes 6 servings.

A Giant Grinder

Even guests who can't cook will be able to pull off this entrée. Pick up several loaves of French bread (or custom order a 4-foot sandwich loaf from your grocery store bakery), cheeses, deli meats, lettuce, and tomatoes on the way to the party. It will take only a few minutes to split open the bread, pile on the sandwich fillings, and cut the sub into individual servings. Guests can then spread on their favorite condiments.

Peanut Butter and Jelly Stars

To kids, potlucks often feature dozens of mystery casseroles, so a stack of star-studded PB & J's can be a welcome sight on the buffet table. Simply use a cookie cutter to cut a bunch of stars (or other fun shapes) from a half dozen sandwiches and then pile the cutouts on a decorative plate.

Cupcake Cones

    24 flat-bottomed ice-cream cones
    1 18.25-ounce package cake mix
    2 cups frosting
    Candy jimmies

Make the cupcakes by filling the ice-cream cones halfway with cake batter (no further or they will not cook thoroughly). Place each cone in a mini cupcake baking tin for stability. Bake at the recommended temperature for about

Cupcake Cone

the same time as cupcakes. Using a pastry bag with a star tip, swirl the frosting on the cone like soft-serve ice cream and sprinkle on jimmies.

Potluck Art

SUCCESSFUL POTLUCKS offer more than just food. They also serve up activities, like a kids' art show, to liven up the party. Suggest a theme, such as Under the Sea or Old McDonald's Farm, and invite the kids to draw pictures before dinner. Then display the drawings for everyone to enjoy. Later, award all the artists a small prize to take home, such as stickers or a pin-on button.

Potluck Art

Christmas Carnival,
page 206

Chapter Six

Holiday Cheer

New Year's Eve ★ Valentine Workshop ★ Easter Party
Fourth of July ★ Halloween Party ★ Thanksgiving Feast
Christmas Carnival ★ Hanukkah Party

WITH ALL the excitement in the air, the holidays are a natural time to entertain. Our homes are dressed in their holiday best — jack-o'-lanterns line our porches on Halloween, tiny white lights brighten our windows on Christmas, and American flags sway over our front lawns on the Fourth of July. We get to indulge in our favorite holiday foods, from pumpkin pies on Thanksgiving to potato latkes on Hanukkah. And our homes are filled with friends and out-of-town relatives who are all in the party spirit.

So let the celebrations begin. In this chapter, we showcase eight party plans for all the major holidays of the year, from New Year's Eve to Hanukkah. You can host your party the weekend before the holiday with friends and neighbors — or work the party games, crafts, and foods into your family's private celebration.

Don't say we didn't warn you: if you try a few of our ideas this year, your kids may insist that you repeat them again next year. Thus a *FamilyFun* holiday tradition will begin.

Get into the holiday spirit: Kick off the holiday season by gathering with friends to prepare for the big day. You might decorate your house for Christmas at a tree-trimming party or help kids make cards at a valentine workshop. These get-togethers will give your family the chance to slow down, visit with friends, and heighten holiday cheer.

Turn a family gathering into a party: When your extended family arrives for Thanksgiving, Easter, or

Holiday Cheer

The Best of the Holidays

FamilyFun contributor Maggie Megaw found a festive way to organize her daughter's birthday party: she borrowed an activity from all the holidays of the year. The kids wore Halloween costumes, trimmed a Christmas tree, dyed Easter eggs, and sat down to a Thanksgiving feast.

Christmas, make the day extra special by planning games, crafts, or activities to precede or follow the meal. You might host an egg hunt on Easter or play a round of Colonial games on Thanksgiving. These activities can help make the time your kids get to spend with faraway relatives all the more memorable.

Make holiday parties hands-on: While parents are busy socializing, keep little hands occupied with a simple holiday craft, such as decorating Christmas cookies or making New Year's hats. Get older kids into the act by asking them to supervise the activity. The party crafts or foods make excellent take-home favors, too.

Create a festive atmosphere: To promote the holiday spirit, play music, such as a spooky sound track for a Halloween party or carols at a Christmas carnival. You might also greet guests at the door in costume, donning a Pilgrim hat for Thanksgiving or a red, white, and blue crown on the Fourth of July.

Deck your halls: A few jack-o'-lanterns, a Christmas tree, or an American flag may be all it takes to spruce up your home for a holiday party. Ask your kids to help you hang balloons and streamers in the holiday theme colors, too. Note: If you plan on hosting the same party next year, store your decorations in clearly labeled boxes. You might also stock up on decorations, which are often discounted the day after the holiday.

Don't overdo it: A party during the holidays can be a hit just by offering good food and good fellowship. So keep things simple. Use the holiday decorations you already have in place, serve dessert instead of a sit-down dinner, or phone friends to invite them to your party rather than sending out handcrafted invitations.

Halloween Party, page 194

New Year's Eve

ON NEW YEAR'S EVE, have a ball with your kids and your friends — without ever leaving your home. With this party plan, you can time the festivities to begin well before midnight, allowing even the youngest revelers to join in. So invite a group of friends to put on silly hats, blow party horns, raise glasses, and toast to a happy New Year.

Timely Decor

TO DECORATE your house for a party on the last day of the year, don't hold back. Start with streamers, balloons, and Happy New Year banners, then litter the floor with confetti. Homemade hats and noise-makers are a must, too. To play up the countdown to midnight, pull out all your ticking clocks (shift midnight to an earlier hour if you'd like little ones to hit the sack early) and draw clock faces on all your balloons.

Cocktail Shakers

New Year's Eve

A Penny for Your Peas

On January 1st, Southerners like to fill up on greens and Hoppin' John — a delicious dish of black-eyed peas and rice. Some say each pea eaten represents a dollar to be gained in the upcoming year.

Party Drinks

WHEN ALL YOUR guests have arrived, toast to the New Year with a colorful cocktail.

New Year's Sunrise

4 ounces seltzer
6 ounces orange juice
½ ounce grenadine syrup
1 orange slice
1 lemon slice
1 Maraschino cherry
Plastic toothpick

In a tall glass, mix the seltzer and orange juice. Slowly pour the grenadine into the center of the glass, allowing the syrup to settle on the bottom (which it does thanks to its greater density). Garnish with the orange, lemon, and cherry, stacked and skewered with the toothpick. Serves 1.

Triple-Red Shirley Temple

1 ounce grenadine syrup
6 ounces cranberry juice
4 ounces cranberry ginger ale
1 paper umbrella
3 Maraschino cherries
½ orange slice
Ice (optional)

Mix the syrup, cranberry juice, and ginger ale in a tall glass. Open the umbrella and slide the cherries on the handle. Balance the umbrella on the glass rim in front of the orange slice. Serves 1.

Starry, Starry Night

4 ounces papaya juice
2 ounces pineapple juice
4 ounces ginger ale
Lemon and lime peel
1 or 2 slices of star fruit
Ice (optional)

In a tall glass, mix the papaya and pineapple juices and the ginger ale. For the garnish, use a small, star-shaped cookie cutter to cut star shapes from the lemon and lime peels. Slide the slices of star fruit onto the glass rim. Serves 1.

Party Hats

A NEW YEAR'S bash calls for outrageous party hats. So set up a table with construction paper, glue, glitter, markers, and other craft supplies and let guests create their own. They can start with a crown, cone, or classic newspaper hat, then build from there, gluing on ornate ribbons, pom-poms, or feathers.

Cocktail Shakers

I N THE HOUR before midnight, keep young revelers busy assembling these simple noisemakers. The rattles are conveniently fashioned from the clear plastic cocktail glasses that people often have on hand during the holidays. To make the shakers, pour a generous handful of beans, rice, buttons, or colorful beads into a cocktail glass. Place another glass on top and, matching them rim to rim, tape the

Cocktail Shakers

two together securely with colorful electrical tape. Now shake the rattles all about.

Stocking Up on Resolutions

I will do the dishes without being asked.

I will eat more fruits and vegetables

Just as fun as making New Year's resolutions is seeing how close you did — or didn't — come to keeping them the year before. For a fun party activity, have guests write out their resolutions on slips of paper (and make predictions for their friends, too). Party guests can take the slips home and follow the lead of the Edgerley family, *FamilyFun* readers in Granville, Illinois. Every year, mom Mary, dad Philip, Emily, 12, Rachel, ten, and Philip, nine, pen their resolutions on New Year's Eve, then tuck them into their Christmas stockings before they're packed away. When the stockings come out of storage the next year, the kids pluck out the lists and put them aside until New Year's Eve when they are shared out loud and replaced with new ones. "It gives you something to look forward to," says Emily.

New Year's Eve

The Bubble Wrap Stomp

Countdown to Midnight

THE BEST COMMOTION on New Year's Eve comes not from the party horns but from excited kids. That's why *FamilyFun* reader Susan Mathews of Minnetonka, Minnesota, developed these countdown cards. During your party, invite the kids to decorate poster board cards by drawing and coloring in the numbers 1 through 10. At midnight, each child should promenade down a flight of steps, number card held high, as the crowd yells out the number. As the last child hits the steps, the steamers should be blowing, the shakers shaking, and the cameras flashing.

The Bubble Wrap Stomp

HANDHELD SHAKERS are perfect for ringing (or rattling) in the New Year, but what if you want to guarantee that your entire party crowd is on its feet and dancing when the clock strikes midnight? Look no further than a packaging supply store. For just a few dollars, says *FamilyFun* reader Elaine Snyder of Jupiter, Florida, you can pick up several yards of the large-bubbled Bubble Wrap used for shipping packages. (Or, simply recycle the Bubble Wrap that comes with holiday gifts.) Just before midnight, unroll the wrap on a hard surface, such as a wooden floor or driveway. When the New Year's countdown concludes, your party guests can do the Bubble Wrap Stomp.

Can't Wait Till the Midnight Hour?

One advantage of making merry at home is that families with young children can perform some magic and shift midnight to an earlier hour. That way, sleepiness (and all that comes with it) won't undermine the celebration. Here are some fun ways to fool the clock.

☛ Gather all your alarm clocks and set them to go off at a designated time.

☛ Select one candle to be your timekeeper. When it burns down to the quick, the big hour has arrived.

☛ Set a kitchen timer for 30 minutes and turn off all the electric lights. By candlelight, talk about your hopes and resolutions for the year to come. When the bell rings, it's midnight, and everyone flips the lights back on and toasts to the New Year.

Confetti Balloons

Confetti Balloons

BALLOONS ARE A MUST for a New Year's party with older kids. Not only do they make a big bang when popped at midnight, but — if they're filled with homemade confetti — they also make a festive and absolutely thrilling mess.

To prepare a batch of balloons for your party, set the kids to work punching circles out of brightly colored construction paper with a hole punch (if they aren't quickly captivated by this simple tool, have some store-bought confetti on hand as a backup).

Next, stuff the confetti into deflated balloons using a funnel. If you don't have a funnel, a plastic soda bottle cut in half works fine. For a twist, have the children write fortunes on small pieces of paper and slip them into the mix.

Blow up the balloons and hang them high, but still within reach of the children. A few moments before the appointed hour, hand each child a pin and, on the stroke of midnight, let the confetti fly.

Holiday Cheer

Rock Around the Clock

To count down to New Year's, the Parmentiers, *FamilyFun* readers in Hudson, New York, host a clock party. Each guest brings an alarm clock, sets it to ring at midnight, and places it on the party table alongside confetti-filled balloons with clock faces. After painting their own faces, kids search for a ticking clock hidden in a room and play "mouse ran up the clock." (To play, a designated "grandfather clock" turns his back to the group and calls out an hour, and the "mice" race to take that number of steps before he turns around. Those who fail return to the starting line. The first mouse to "run up" the clock wins.) At midnight, the alarms ring, balloons pop, and everyone celebrates.

Clock Face-Painting

Valentine Workshop

VALENTINE'S DAY, as far as kids are concerned, doesn't call for roses and champagne. To them, saying "I Love You" means crafting silly cards, eating sweet stuff, and playing red-hot games. On February 14th, invite a group of mushballs under 12 to join in this kid-style celebration of love.

Sweet Nothing Invitations

SEND THIS sweet party messenger — a butterfly valentine invitation — to all your friends. To make one, place shoestring licorice "antennae" between two pieces of stick gum, taping the top and bottom closed to secure the antennae in place. Next cut two heart-shaped wings from construction paper, and write "Happy Valentine's Day" on the front and the party details on the back. Secure the wings in place with a heart sticker. Give the butterfly a face with more heart stickers.

Lovely Decor

ON VALENTINE'S DAY, your house should look as cute as Cupid. Start by outfitting the party room with balloons and streamers in the official colors of love — pink, white, and red. Tape construction paper hearts with romantic sayings to the walls. Finally, dress up the craft and lunch tables with red paper tablecloths, adding a bowl of conversation hearts in the center for nibbling.

Heart-Shaped Animal Masks

LOVE CAN COME in many disguises, as *FamilyFun* reader Lindy Schneider of Bozeman, Montana, and her family prove with these animal masks. (At the heart of each mask is — a heart!) Before your party, cut a pair of hearts from white poster board, making them large enough to cover a child's face. Carefully cut out eyeholes. Glue the two pieces together, sandwiching a tongue depressor or paint stirrer between them. Using this basic shape, invite guests to add elements to make various animal masks. To make the panda pictured at left, tape on paper ears and eyes, a heart nose, and a pink tongue.

Heart-Shaped Animal Mask

Heart Hunt

Valentine Workshop

Hunt for a Romantic Rock

Hold a family treasure hunt for heart-shaped rocks in the stoniest places near you: try a stream bank, a driveway, or the parking lot. The rocks don't have to be perfect — just close enough to paint rosy red for a sweetheart.

Red-Hot Games

KEEP SPIRITS HIGH at your party with a round of Valentine's Day games. Here are four simple ones you can choose from.

Heart Hunt: For little kids, stage a heart hunt, planting conversation hearts (or construction paper hearts) all around the house. The object: Have the kids find as many hearts as they can.

The And Game: This word game is just right for Valentine's Day. It's called The And Game since it's all about words that appear together with *and* in between. I say, "Romeo and …"

Spin Art Heart

You say, "Juliet." I say, "Bread and …" You have to come up with "butter." After five, switch roles.

Kind Things: Here's a good game for siblings. Set the timer and see how many kind things you can write down about a person in, say, 3 minutes. You might suggest writing down generous things the person has done or nice things about the way he or she acts, thinks, plays, works, or looks. Done right, this game will clear the air of sibling rivalry for the afternoon.

Hearts: Remember that card game where you either avoid winning any hearts or "shoot the moon" and collect all of them? Hearts is a great one for today. If you don't already know how to play it, you can find the directions in a card game book.

Valentine Crafts

INVITE GUESTS to get a little crafty — and romantic — by making these valentines to take home.

Spin Art Hearts: Put a new spin on the traditional valentine with this salad spinner art sent in by Kellie Weenink, a *FamilyFun* reader in Parma, Ohio. First line the bottom of an old salad spinner with a paper plate. Pour small amounts of red, pink, and purple liquid tempera paint on the plate's surface, close the spinner's top, and whirl away. Remove the plate. Once the paint is dry, cut it into a heart shape (use novelty craft scissors for a different edge). Write a poem or saying on the back and give it to your heart's desire.

Lollipop Mice: These whiskered sweet nothings tote along lollipops, making them the perfect valentines to give to pint-size suckers for love. Since these cards — just like real mice — are easily multiplied, they're a good bet for

Hearts

classrooms and play groups.

From stiff colored paper, cut out a bunch of hearts, about 4 inches across. On each, draw a nose and eyes. Punch four holes above the mouse's nose. Thread a short length of pipe cleaner through the top two holes and another through the bottom two. Lastly, slip a lollipop (either flat or round) down behind the whiskers.

A Lovely Menu

T HE FASTEST way to your guests' hearts may be through their stomachs. Hence, your Valentine's Day party foods should be littered with expressions of affection. Serve heart-shaped sandwiches (cut with a cookie cutter) or pizza (shape pizza dough into a heart) along with Love Potion and Painted Heart Cookies.

Love Potion

    ½ cup frozen strawberries
    ½ cup frozen raspberries
    1 cup white grape or apple juice
    Maraschino cherries

Lollipop Mice

Slightly thaw the strawberries and raspberries, then place them in a blender along with the juice. Mix on high until you have a uniform color. Garnish with cherries. Serves 2.

Painted Heart Cookies

With edible paint, you can turn an old staple — heart-shaped cookies — into valentine canvases. First mix up your favorite sugar cookie recipe, cut out the heart shapes, and refrigerate until ready to paint and bake. To make each color of paint, mix 1 egg yolk and ¼ teaspoon water. Add a few drops of food coloring until you've reached the desired shade. Using a clean paintbrush, paint onto the uncooked sugar cookie dough, then bake according to recipe directions.

Love Potion and
Painted Heart Cookies

Tiny Treat Bags

Each year the Graham kids, *FamilyFun* readers in Pleasant Grove, Utah, design, package, and label a card-and-treat-in-one valentine for classmates. For the labels, they use rubber stamps on card stock, then they fill small plastic bags with valentine candies. They seal them with a staple — and a kiss.

Easter Party

THE MAGIC OF EASTER lies not only in the religious traditions but also in the excitement of a new season. With the scent of spring comes renewal — fresh greenery, warm breezes, and tulips in the yard. This Easter, invite friends and family to celebrate all things spring by dressing up like bunny rabbits, nibbling on carrot cake, and running around the yard in an eggs-traordinary egg hunt.

Spring Invitations

Spring Invitations

FOR SIMPLE, inexpensive invitations, have your kids trace cookie-cutter shapes of chicks or rabbits onto construction paper and decorate them with markers and stick-ers. Besides mentioning the obvious, like when to come (perhaps from 2 to 4 P.M.), ask guests to wear spring clothes — Easter hats optional.

Decorations

Tulips, daffodils, and other early bloomers will go a long way toward sprucing up your house for an Easter party. For extra credit, hang pastel balloons on your walk-way and a dec-orated card-board egg on your door.

Bunny Disguises

Bunny Bag

Easter Egg Hunt

A FEW DAYS BEFORE your party, fill plastic eggs with small toys, jelly beans, and wrapped candies — about 12 eggs per party guest. On the morning of the party, hide all the plastic eggs for the hunt. You may want to divide your yard into two areas — the front yard for the youngest children to hunt in and the backyard for the older kids. Hide the eggs for the younger crowd in low branches, soft, open places, and easy-to-reach crannies. For the older kids, show no mercy when hiding the eggs. Tuck them in pipes, under leaves, and around corners.

Along with the plastic eggs, hide a few special, decorative eggs in difficult-to-find spots. These eggs are not the prizes, but chits the lucky finders carry to the host, who then exchanges them for chocolate bunnies, sugared eggs, or, if you're sugar averse, stuffed animals or Peter Rabbit books.

At the sound of the whistle, send the kids scurrying for Easter eggs. The hunt ends when the last egg is uncovered.

Bunny Bags

IF PARTY GUESTS are going to put all their Easter eggs in one basket, this big-eared Bunny Bag is the one. As guests arrive, invite them to make bags for collecting eggs during the hunt. Begin by cutting a U shape about 4 inches deep down the middle of the top of a paper lunch bag (while holding it closed). Open the bag and cut the sides down even with the bottom of the U. Glue the resulting flaps together, front to back, to create ear loop handles. Glue on two googly eyes. Cut ear, whisker, and teeth shapes from construction paper and glue them on, as shown. Finally, add a cotton ball nose and a cotton tail.

Margie Luttrell's Annual Egg Hunt

Every Easter, a swarm of 50 kids scatters in *FamilyFun* reader Margie Luttrell's yard in Knoxville, Tennessee, scouting for Easter eggs under bushes, down paths, and beneath stones. Beforehand, Margie and a couple of friends fill some 2,000 plastic eggs with candy and prizes and hide half in the front yard for the little kids and the other half in the backyard for the big kids. Friends bring their own baskets and food to share. Margie likes to start the hunt after the guests have sampled the food and the children have begun to paw the ground like racehorses. Then the countdown begins, and egg mania erupts.

Easter Party

Bunny Disguises

Bunny Nose

AN EASTER PARTY need not be a formal affair, but a few guests may want to wear tails — not to mention ears and noses. Here's how to make them.

Bunny Nose: Cut a cup from an egg carton, leaving a tab of extra material on one side for teeth. Trim the cup's edges and paint the teeth white,

Bunny Tail: Form batting into a cottontail, then sew a length of yarn through it with an embroidery needle. Tie the yarn around your child's waist.

Easter Plates

HERE'S AN ESPECIALLY festive, and disposable, party plate to hold all your rabbit chow, from spring veggies and dip to the Mr. McGregor's Garden Cake at right.

To make one party plate, cut two semicircular ear shapes from the sides of a paper plate. Staple them to the back of another plate, as shown. Make four cuts down the side of a muffin cup and fold two sections to the center to create a bow tie. Staple in place. Add jelly bean eyes. Cut whiskers from a third, smaller plate and teeth from white paper. Place them in the center of the plate with a chocolate kiss nose (until the food is served).

Bunny Disguises

drawing a black gap between them. Glue on a pom-pom nose. For whiskers, cut pipe cleaners into three pieces. Poke three holes on either side of the nose with a pencil, then feed the pipe cleaner whiskers through the holes. Make air vents with a hole punch along the cup's bottom. Keep the nose on tight with an elastic band knotted through holes poked in the cup's sides.

Bunny Ears: Cut out the edges of the egg carton top and glue them to a headband with a glue gun (parents only).

Bunny Ears

Easter Plate

Mr. McGregor's Garden Cake

LIKE HIS COUSIN Peter Rabbit, the Easter Bunny has been known to steal vegetables from Mr. McGregor's patch. On this garden carrot cake, the almond Easter Bunny nibbles marzipan cabbages, carrots, and radishes.

CARROT CAKE:

 3 eggs
 1¼ cups corn oil
 1⅓ cups packed brown sugar
 2 teaspoons baking soda
 2 teaspoons cinnamon
 ½ teaspoon salt
 2 cups all-purpose flour
 1 8-ounce can crushed pineapple in natural syrup
 ⅓ cup shredded coconut
 1 cup coarsely chopped walnuts
 3 cups grated carrots (about 4 carrots)

CREAM CHEESE FROSTING:

 ½ cup unsalted butter, softened to room temperature
 ½ cup cream cheese, softened to room temperature
 2½ to 3 cups sifted confectioners' sugar
 1 tablespoon fresh lemon juice
 Green food coloring

DECORATIONS:

 3 tablespoons crushed chocolate cookies
 Marzipan rabbits and vegetables (see recipe at right)

To make the carrot cake, preheat the oven to 350°. Grease and flour a 13- by 9- by 2-inch pan. In a large bowl, beat the eggs, oil, and brown sugar until well blended. In a separate bowl, sift the

Mr. McGregor's Garden Cake

baking soda, cinnamon, salt, and flour, then gradually add it to the egg mixture; do not overmix. Add the pineapple and syrup, coconut, walnuts, and carrots, and beat well.

Pour the batter into the prepared pan and bake for 45 to 55 minutes, or until a toothpick inserted in the center comes out clean. Cool in the pan for 10 to 15 minutes. Invert onto a cooling rack and cool completely.

Meanwhile, mix up the cream cheese frosting. In the bowl of an electric mixer, cream the butter and cream cheese until fluffy. Add the remaining frosting ingredients and beat until smooth.

Ice the cooled cake and sprinkle the crushed cookies on top for "dirt." Add the bunnies and rows of marzipan vegetables. Serves 12 to 14.

Marzipan Decorations

To make the cake decorations, break about 14 ounces of marzipan into balls and knead in dabs of food coloring paste, leaving a few balls uncolored for the bunnies. Next mold the marzipan like clay into orange carrots with green tops, red cabbage, green lettuce, red radishes, and white Flopsy, Mopsy, and Cottontail.

Fourth of July

INDEPENDENCE DAY was the first date to be declared an American holiday, preceding even Thanksgiving. From the start, it sparked unbridled revels with ship cannon salutes, resounding bells, and firecrackers. In this party, we're following those time-honored leads, kicking off July with a day full of high-spirited relay races, a homespun parade, and a feast of summertime foods.

PARTY STATS

Ages: All
Size: 10 to 40 guests
Length: 2 to 4 hours
Prep time: 2 hours
Cost: $4 per guest

Patriotic Spirit

Over the years, communities have come up with unique ways of celebrating the Fourth of July. Since 1818, the townsfolk of Lititz, Pennsylvania, have illuminated the local park with 7,000 candles. In the 1940s, a two-mile-long picnic table bordered the parade route in Ontario, California. And today on the streets of Bristol, Rhode Island, red, white, and blue stripes replace the yellow traffic lines.

A Grand Old Parade

FOURTH OF JULY parades have been a tradition since the Liberty Bell rang in 1776. Start your party by participating in a local parade or staging your own neighborhood event. Festive hats, makeshift drums, and an independence banner will get the holiday march off on the right foot.

Before the party, make a parade banner on a large sheet of butcher paper. With red and blue markers, write "Happy Independence Day." When guests arrive, have them sign in by adding their names to the mural. Once everyone is accounted for and the sign is complete, elect two people to hold the banner and lead the parade.

Distribute whatever musical instruments you have on hand, including drums, kazoos, pots, pans, and spoons. When the orchestra is assembled, set up a portable stereo or boom box and crank up "Yankee Doodle," "The Stars and Stripes Forever," and so on, encouraging everyone to play and parade around.

Parade Banner

Firecracker Hats

WITH THIS QUICK and inexpensive design, you can easily outfit a crowd of paraders with hats that will flutter as they march.

First unfold two full sheets of newspaper one atop the other as if you were reading them. From here, treat them as a single two-ply sheet.

To make the brow band, use a ruler to mark a line that measures 3½ inches from the bottom edge of the sheet and fold up along that line. Roll the band up once more and flatten the fold. Paint the brow band blue. When dry, paint broad red and white stripes on the flip side of the newspaper (this will be the inside of the hat). While waiting for the paint to dry, cut star shapes from white construction paper.

Fit the hat by wrapping the brow band (painted side out) around a child's head and taping the overlap securely. At this point, the hat should resemble a tall cylinder. Decorate the brow by gluing on the white stars. Finally, use scissors to fringe the top of the hat, making cuts (an inch apart) that extend halfway down the cylinder.

Coffee Can Drum

Firecracker Hat

Coffee Can Drums

KIDS MARCH to a different drummer when banging on these crafty cans. To make one, use white paint to decorate a piece of red construction paper with stars. Then invert an empty coffee can and wrap and glue the paper around it, leaving an inch of overhang for fringe. Punch two holes into the can's sides with a nail (a parent's job) and string with ribbon. Now grab wooden spoon drumsticks and let the marching band begin.

Flag Face-Painting

Show your patriotic streak at the Fourth of July parade by dabbing on red, white, and blue face paint. Use water-based face paint to draw a flag, complete with stars and stripes, over your child's cheeks, nose, and forehead.

Fourth of July

Egg and Wooden Spoon Race

Stars and Stripes T-Shirts

Set up an area where kids can decorate star-spangled T-shirts. On a picnic table covered with newspaper, set out white T-shirts, cardboard, star fruit (or potato star stamps), and red and blue fabric paint. Insert the cardboard inside the T-shirts to create a flat surface. Then pour the paint into pie tins. Slice the star fruit in half and dry the cut surfaces with paper towels. Dip the fruit (or potato) into the paint and press stars on the shirt. To heat-set the design, follow package instructions.

Balloon Brigade

THIS FAST-PACED race lets winners go out with a real bang. Before the start, each team assembles in single file with the first player in each line holding a balloon.

Balloon Brigade

When the whistle blows, each lead player passes the balloon between her legs to the next person in line. Each recipient in turn passes the balloon overhead to the teammate directly behind her. The balloon is passed alternately between players' legs and over players' heads all the way down the line. When the last person receives the balloon, he or she races to the front of the line and the balloon pass resumes. The relay continues until one of the original lead players regains position at the front of her line and pops the team balloon.

Egg and Wooden Spoon Race

FEW HARD-BOILED eggs (either plain or decorated), two wooden spoons, and two team flags are needed for this relay. Each team stands in single file behind the starting line and opposite their respective flags, set in the ground about 5 yards away. At the whistle, the first player in each line, balancing an egg on a spoon, races around his team's flag, then back to transfer the egg and the spoon to the next teammate. The recipient races to the flag, and the race continues until one team finishes the course. Anyone who drops an egg must run to the start line for another before resuming.

Popcorn Relay

Popcorn Relay

F ANCY FOOTWORK is the ticket to success in this event, which is as much fun to watch as it is to run in. Beforehand, prepare a pair of plastic or paper cups for each runner. Use a tack to poke a hole in the center of each cup bottom. Push one end of a thick rubber band through the hole and into the cup. Then slip a paper clip on the end of the band inside the cup, and gently pull the other end until the clip rests on the bottom of the cup. The rubber band, worn around the foot, holds the cup in place atop the shoe.

Just prior to the race, a member from each team is issued a big bag of popcorn and charged with filling teammates' cups from the moment the starting whistle blows until the relay ends. These individuals stand alongside their teams behind the starting line. Two large, shallow boxes are set 5 yards beyond the starting line, opposite the teams.

When the whistle blows, the first person in each line gets his cups filled, sprints to the team box, and empties his cups into it, trying to lose as little popcorn as possible along the way. He then runs back to tag the next person in line. The new runner heads to the team box, and the first runner goes to the end of the line. The relay continues for 2 minutes, or until one of the popcorn bags is emptied. Then the popcorn in each box is measured, and the team with the most is declared the winner.

Ring Toss

Ring Toss

FOR THIS GAME, contestants need the tossing skills of a Frisbee player and the good aim of a seasoned horseshoe pitcher.

For the scoring poles, you'll need nine dowels. Set them in the ground in three rows, each composed of three dowels and spaced 2 feet apart. Decorate the planted poles by wrapping them with red, white, and blue crepe paper streamers.

For the rings (three per team), use a dozen sturdy paper plates. You can either purchase colored plates or spray-paint plain ones. Cut out a large circle from the center of each plate. Then place two of the plates face to face and tape them together all the way around the rims. Repeat to make five more rings.

During the game, members from both teams have three attempts each to toss a ring around one of the poles. (It's fun to alternate turns between the two teams.) Kids should be allowed to stand a little closer to the poles than their adult teammates.

A ring that lands around a pole in the nearest row is worth 10 points; a ringer in the middle row earns 20 points; a ringer in the far row earns 30 points. The team that accumulates the most points wins.

Red, White, & Blueberry Shortcake

Fourth of July Float

If you're going to raise a toast to the Stars and Stripes, you'll want to do it with something dazzling and delicious — like this red, white, and blueberry float. Fill a tall, frosty glass three quarters of the way with raspberry soda. Float a large scoop of vanilla ice cream on top and garnish with a handful of blueberries and a strawberry, festive decorations, and an American flag. Serve with a straw and a long spoon.

Red, White, & Blueberry Shortcake

THIS RECIPE MIXES up the best of the red, white, and blue — fresh strawberries, blueberries, and whipped cream spooned over shortcake.

    5 cups all-purpose flour
    4 teaspoons baking powder
    ½ teaspoon salt
    1 teaspoon nutmeg
    ¼ cup sugar
    ½ cup margarine or shortening
    2 cups milk
    2 quarts fresh strawberries, sliced
    ½ cup sugar
    1 pint whipping cream
    2 tablespoons maple syrup
    1 pint fresh blueberries

Preheat the oven to 425°. Sift the flour, baking powder, salt, nutmeg, and ¼ cup of sugar in a large bowl. Using a pastry cutter, mix the margarine and dry ingredients until they resemble a coarse meal. Stir in the milk until the mixture holds together. Turn the dough onto a floured surface and pat it into a 1-inch-thick circle. Use a biscuit cutter to cut out the shortcakes. Arrange them 1½ inches apart on an ungreased baking sheet. Bake for 10 to 12 minutes.

Place the sliced strawberries in a large bowl. Sprinkle with the ½ cup of sugar. Stir, cover, and refrigerate until the berries release juices and make a syrup. Next use an electric mixer to whip the cream and maple syrup in a chilled stainless steel bowl.

To assemble, split the biscuits in half. Spoon the strawberries and syrup onto the bottoms. Cover with the remaining shortcake halves and spoon more of the strawberries on top. Top with the whipped cream and garnish with fresh blueberries. Serves 10 to 12.

Fourth of July Float

Halloween Party

HALLOWEEN HAS ALWAYS been one of our favorite holidays. The problem is, after all that costume-making, decorating, and anticipation, it's over in a one-hour trick-or-treat spree. With this party, you can make the holiday last much longer. Invite friends to show off their costumes, gobble creepy cuisine, and play wickedly fun games — they'll take home lots of memories along with their candy hoard.

PARTY STATS

Ages: All
Size: 8 to 20 guests
Length: 2 hours
Prep time: 3 hours
Cost: $4 per guest

Haunting Your House

Besides creepy jack-o'-lanterns, every haunted house should have any of the following:

☛ **A spooky sound track**
☛ **Fake spiderwebs**
☛ **Plastic insects**
☛ **Monster footprints (cut from poster board or sponge-painted)**
☛ **A mummy-wrapped scarecrow**
☛ **Dead flowers**
☛ **Furniture covered with sheets**
☛ **Black lights (shining on glow-in-the-dark creatures)**
☛ **Helium balloon ghosts (drape balloons with sheets and tie at the neck)**
☛ **Cardboard box coffin**

Velcome to our Haunted House

A FEW WEEKS before your Halloween bash, phone friends and invite them to come to your diabolical mansion, dressed in costume, on Halloween Eve or the weekend before or after fright night.

Spooky Decor

MOODY LIGHTING, haunting music, and a few well-placed homemade decorations set the scene for your Halloween bash. Avoid anything with a flame and keep in mind that costumes make kids clumsy — anything fragile or sharp should be moved. Here are a few decorations to get you started.

Giggly Gravestones: It's a not-so-grave sight when guests step into a silly cemetery in your front yard. Cut gravestones out of cardboard, paint them gray, and inscribe them with funny epitaphs, such as Scared E. Cat. On the night of the party, attach garden stakes to the backs of the stones with duct tape and plant them in the yard, tipping some at odd angles for that seventeenth-century look. Partly bury a hat or boots in the front of each stone, so it looks as if the deceased may rise to the occasion.

Furry Spiders: A doorway web filled with furry arachnids is sure to stop guests in their tracks. For each spider, you'll need four pipe cleaners, a four-hole button, and a pair of stick-on googly eyes. To begin, bend a pipe cleaner into a V shape. Push the base of the V up through one of the button holes until it protrudes ½ inch. Then bend the ½-inch length over the top of the button. Use the same method to thread the three other pipe cleaners through the remaining button holes.

Next shape the eight legs by bending the pipe cleaner ends first 1 inch from the button and then again ¼ inch from the tips. Stick the googly eyes onto the button between the front legs. For a web, use a synthetic stretching spiderweb (sold at most novelty shops for under $2). Then set your spiders in the web wherever you like — their legs will stick easily to the fibers.

Furry Spiders

Spooky Decor

Halloween Party

Frightening Fun

AT YOUR HALLOWEEN bash, plan more events than you think you need (and some for bad weather, too). In addition to the following games, prepare easy backups: bobbing for apples, painting Halloween murals or pumpkins, or dancing to spooky sounds.

Costume Parade: When all the guests have arrived, organize a terror-raising march in the backyard or around the block to show off everyone's ghoulish gear. Turn on a spooky sound track to start the march — and don't forget to take photographs.

Pin the Wart on the Witch: Hang a picture of a witch at kid's-eye level on the wall, then wad up modeling clay into gumball-size "warts." Blindfolded, kids take turns trying to stick the wart on the witch's nose.

The Mummy Wrap: Divide the kids into teams of two, give each pair a roll of toilet paper, and instruct one member of each team to race to wrap his partner, mummy style, at the sound of a screech. Kids must use up the whole roll, avoiding the head and wrapping arms separately from the torso. Once wrapped, the mummy yells "mummy wrap!" Award the winning team, reverse partners' roles, and start again.

Boo Am I? To put a frenzied twist on a traditional game of charades, write out clues for Halloween characters on slips of paper (Frankenstein, a mummy, a mad scientist, Dracula, a skeleton, a cat, a bat, a rat, and so on). Put each slip inside white "ghost" balloons, blow up the balloons, and set them aside. Divide the kids into two teams. The first player has three minutes to choose a balloon, pop it, read the clue inside, and silently act it out until her team guesses the clue. The child to guess correctly picks the next balloon.

Eyeball Relay: Before the party, make the eyeballs (you'll need at least six for each team). Use colored markers to draw irises, pupils, and bloodshot veins on Ping-Pong balls. To play, set a chair across the room from each team. Have the first player on each team cup his hands and fill them with eyeballs. On cue, those players must race around their team's chair and back to hand off their eyeballs to the next teammate in line. Eyeballs that are dropped in the transfer must be retrieved before the second runner can head for the chair. The first team whose members all complete the course wins.

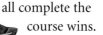

Eyeball Relay

Costume Parade

Ghost Storytelling: In a jack-o'-lantern-lit room, a ghost (parent in costume) gathers storytellers into a circle and starts spinning a spooky yarn into a handheld tape recorder: "One night, Mr. Bonapart heard the sound of heavy footsteps in his attic. With every step, the house rattled …" She then passes the tape recorder to a child, who improvises what happened next ("The man couldn't take the noise, so he went upstairs with a bat…"). Once each child has had a chance to speak, the ghost rewinds the tape, and the gang listens to the story. Older kids enjoy the added challenge of pulling an object (a feather, dog collar, mirror, and whatever else you can round up) out of a box and incorporating the item into the story.

Freaky Hair

This activity will make your guests' hair stand on end. Spread out a white sheet on the floor or on a bed, then have a child lie down on it. Help the child fan out his or her hair (have a wig on hand for the crew-cut contingent). Invite the child to make his or her most gruesome Halloween face while you take a Polaroid picture from directly above. When the photo develops, write the child's name on it, use it as a place card for the party table, and then send it home as a party favor.

DEVON

Halloween Party

Spider Pretzels

It's easy to make these arachnid treats, and they look positively lifelike crawling all over the table. Spread two crackers with peanut butter and insert eight pretzel stick legs into

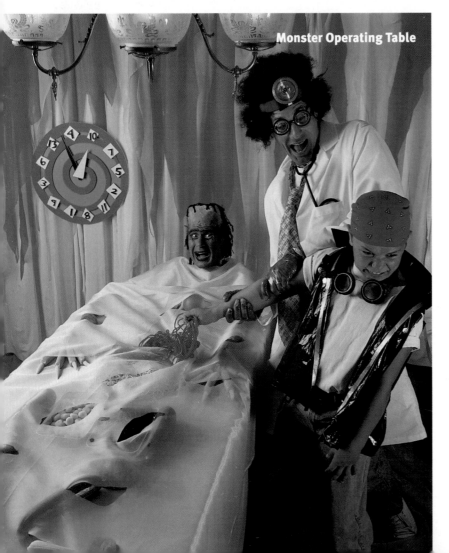

the filling. With a dab of peanut butter, set two raisin eyes on top.

Monster Operating Table:
In this gooey game, a parent made up as a monster sits at the end of an operating table as young physicians (party guests) examine his ghoulish guts. To make the body, arrange food on a picnic table to resemble a skeleton, minus the head (which, after all, belongs to a dad).

For arms, thighs, and shins, use zucchini; a turnip, split in half, makes excellent kneecaps. Use toothpicks to pin a celery rib cage together; secure dried apricot toes to celery feet; and attach baby corn fingernails to hotdog fingers. Just below the rib cage, pile cooked spaghetti (small intestines) and licorice ropes (large intestines). Below the intestines, fill a pie plate with Jell-O (guts). Add water chestnut gallstones and a water balloon heart.

Monster Operating Table

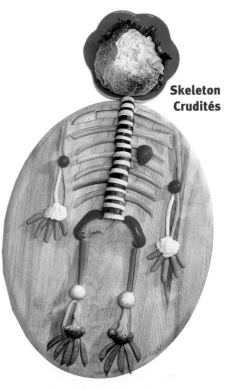

Skeleton Crudités

When the organs are in place, secure them to the table with duct tape. Top with an old sheet and cut slits so the kids can reach in and touch the organs without being able to see them. Next position the live monster as close to the head of the table as possible, sitting on a chair. To create the illusion that the head is connected to the body, drape a second sheet over the monster's shoulders. Now invite the guests to operate on his guts.

Creepy Cuisine

A HALLOWEEN PARTY cries out for a perfectly inelegant menu. Start with Skeleton Crudités followed by deviled egg sandwiches cut with Halloween cookie cutters. For dessert, serve up the Witch's House Cake.

Skeleton Crudités

To make the vegetable platter, prep the freshest vegetables you can find the day before the party and store them, soaked in water, in the refrigerator. When you're ready, just drain and pat dry, and arrange on a platter as shown above. For a gruesome noggin, fill a cabbage head with your favorite dip for brains.

Witch's House Cake

When guests dig into this devilishy delicious cake, it will be love at first bite.

- 3 baked devil's food cakes: a 13- by 9- by 2-inch, an 8-inch round cake baked in an ovenproof bowl, and a 6-inch loaf
- 4 cups chocolate frosting
- 1 cup orange frosting
  Decorations: green gumdrops, chocolate graham crackers and cones, peanut butter sandwich cookies, black shoestring and twist licorice, chocolate kisses, mini chocolate chips, green hard candies, mini marshmallows, and chocolate-covered raisins

Cover a large cutting board with foil. Place the 13- by 9- by 2-inch cake on top to create the "graveyard." On one end, place the bowl-shaped cake "hill." Ice the graveyard and hill with chocolate frosting. Cut a 2- by 3-inch rectangle, about 1 inch deep, on top of the hill to accommodate the house.

Turn the loaf cake into a house by cutting the corners off one end to form a peaked roof. Place the house in the 2- by 3-inch slot and "paint" with orange frosting. Tile the roof with chocolate graham crackers and frosting. Add scary details: windows made of broken chocolate cones with orange icing grids and a peanut cookie door with a candy doorknob. Surround the house with shoestring licorice barbed wire. Add a flying witch (a gumdrop face with a chocolate kiss hat on a licorice broomstick).

To create gravestones, break peanut cookies in half and pipe on spooky sayings with orange frosting (R.I.P.,

Holiday Cheer

Boo, and so on). Secure in the muddy frosting. Next make ghosts in the trees (cut crooked branches in a piece of licorice and add mini marshmallow ghosts with mini chocolate chip eyes), then plant the trees in the mud. Next draw a crooked path from the base of the cake up to the witch's door with a toothpick. Outline the path with chocolate-covered raisins, then sprinkle with broken green hard candies. At the entrance, add a chocolate graham cracker drawbridge. Finally, outline the yard with broken chocolate cone fencing. Set the house in a place for all to see — and scream about.

Witch's House Cake

Monster Paws

Your kids won't wait to get their hands on these popcorn-stuffed party favors, recommended by *FamilyFun* reader Julie Peters of Lakewood, Colorado. Begin with washed clear plastic gloves (available at beauty supply stores). Stick one candy corn at the tip of each finger, pointy side up, for fingernails. Fill the glove with popcorn. Tie a bow at the wrist with ribbon.

Thanksgiving Feast

THIS THANKSGIVING, mix a little education into your turkey day by throwing a party that is true to our Pilgrim forebears. This Plimoth-inspired collection of old-time crafts, foods, and games will have your family and friends partying like the Pilgrims and the Wampanoag (the Native Americans who attended the first feast).

An Old-Fashioned Dinner Table

Hand-Quilled Place Card

IF YOU WERE setting the table in 1621, you wouldn't put down any forks. Pilgrims used knives, spoons, fingers, and yard-long napkins to eat their food. For your feast, use full table settings — and place cards.

Hand-Quilled Place Cards: For old-fashioned place cards, dip quill pens in ink and write names in fancy letters. To make the quill, use a pen to outline a triangle, with a sharp tip, on the base of a store-bought feather. Use an X-Acto knife to cut along the triangle to form the point (parents only). Your child can then dip the pen in ink — frequently — and write names on place cards in her best penmanship.

Thanksgiving Feast

Mayflower Centerpiece:
The original *Mayflower* sailed for 66 days and carried almost 130 people to the New World. This milk carton vessel stays put but also holds important cargo — your friends' and families' list of thanks.

To make one, close and tape shut the opening of a clean half-gallon milk carton, then lay it on its side. Using an X-Acto knife (a parent's job), cut out the side of the carton that's facing up. Cut 1-inch strips from a brown paper bag, dip them into a glue mixture (made from one part white glue and four parts water), and wrap the strips around the carton. Repeat until the carton is covered with panels. Attach white paper sails and colored paper flags to bamboo skewers. Stick the

Mayflower Centerpiece

skewers into an apple and set them into the boat.

When they arrive, invite your guests to write down on paper slips something they're thankful for, such as "I am thankful for Grandpa's homemade cranberry sauce." Fold and place the slips in the *Mayflower* for reading before your Thanksgiving feast.

Hand-Quilled Place Cards

Turkey Bread

WHILE THE real bird is roasting, serve guests this Turkey Bread, filled with a dip made from clams, a common food for the Pilgrims.

Cut the top off a round loaf, hollow out the center, and fill with store-bought clam dip. Slice the loaf top in half for the bird's wings and attach them with toothpicks. To make the head, cut an X in a roll and insert a carrot tip for the nose with a red pepper wattle. Use toothpicks to attach the head and raisin eyes. For "feathers," slice a zucchini, summer squash, and carrot lengthwise into ¼-inch slabs and push into bamboo skewers. For a feathery look, jag the edges, then stick into the bread.

Table for Four

When *FamilyFun* reader Eileen Allen offered to host Thanksgiving at her home in Draper, Utah, her kids were thrilled until they realized they would have to sit at the kids' table. So mom Eileen suggested they decorate it. Brent and Adam wrapped the table legs with crepe paper and then made canvas place mats. Eileen picked up silly straws, candy kisses, and napkin holders. Needless to say, the kids' table was the most popular seat in the house.

Thanksgiving Feast

Hats Off

Last Thanksgiving, *FamilyFun* reader Janelle Gray's Pilgrim hat cupcakes were the hit of her son's Alexandria, Virginia, class. She filled flat-bottomed ice-cream cones halfway with cake mix batter, stood the cones in muffin tins, and baked according to package directions. Once cooled, she turned them over and taped black paper hatbands and yellow buckles to each cone.

Dressing for Dinner

CONJURE UP an image of a Pilgrim, and you'll probably imagine a serious, bearded fellow dressed in black. But actually it was just as common for Pilgrims to wear purples and reds. The Wampanoag, on the other hand, wore deerskin leather clothes and lots of homemade jewelry. For your Thanksgiving feast, invite guests to craft one of these Native American or Pilgrim accessories.

Native American Medallion: All well-dressed Wampanoag (who often sported but a single feather in their hair) wore shell jewelry, as well as carved pendants or medallions bearing symbols that held special meaning for their wearers.

To make a felt medallion to wear at your feast, cut out two circles, each one approximately 4 inches in diameter, from a piece of light brown felt. (For a guideline, trace around the lid of a coffee can with chalk.) Use a single-hole punch (or scissors) to cut out circles around the outside of both pieces of felt, leaving a ¼-inch margin and 2 inches for the opening of the pouch. Place one circle on top of the other, then use an 18-inch piece of yarn to stitch the two felt pieces together. Knot the yarn in the back of the medallion.

Now make a braided chain for the necklace. Twist together two pieces of yellow yarn, two pieces of red, and two pieces of brown (each piece of yarn should be about 1 yard long). You can then braid the three colors together. As you are braiding, you can add wooden beads by tying a knot in the braid, slipping on a ½-inch wooden bead, and then tying another knot on the other side. Thread each end of the braided chain through the top holes on each side of the opening of the pouch and tie the ends together on the back.

Ask your child to come up with a design for the front of the medallion (she can sketch one on a separate sheet of paper first) and then use permanent marker to draw the design on the felt. Remind your child that she should draw something that's meaningful to her or to the person to whom she plans to give the medallion. (She can also write a message and slip it inside the pouch.)

Native American Medallion

Pilgrim's Hat: Pilgrim men wore a variety of hats to protect themselves from the weather but also for pure adornment. It would not be unusual to see a hat with a brightly colored band or a feather tucked inside (belt buckles were an addition of the late seventeenth century). Once an adult has supervised the cutting, a young child can assemble this hat (which requires no sewing) by himself.

Pilgrim's Hat Materials

To make the hat, wrap a 7- by 25-inch rectangle of black felt around your child's head and mark with chalk where the fit is right. Remove the felt and use a glue stick or low-temperature glue gun to attach the ends of the felt at the place you've just marked. Place the hat top in the center of a 13-inch-wide black felt circle and trace around the circumference, leaving about a 3-inch hat brim. Set aside the hat top. Using chalk, divide the circle into eight pie slices or spokes. Cut along the spokes (but do not cut around the outside of the circle) so that you have eight pointed flaps. Slip the felt circle over the hat top, leaving the pointed flaps sticking up. Then fold back each flap and glue them onto the hat top (the top of the hat will be open). Glue on a colored felt band so that it covers the folded-over flaps and add a feather (found at most craft stores).

Pilgrim's Bonnet: Before seventeenth-century women and girls began their workdays, they would put on one of these white coifs (or bonnets) to keep their hair out of the way. Pilgrim women made their coifs out of white linen, but you can just as easily fashion one by folding and sewing a white handkerchief.

To make the bonnet, lay a 16- by 16-inch handkerchief flat on a surface and place a 36-inch white shoelace across the center, so that it divides the handkerchief in half. Fold the handkerchief over the shoelace, and then fold in half again so that you form a square. Sew up the side of the square opposite the shoelace (this will be the back of the bonnet) and then shape into a coif. Use the shoelace to tighten it to fit your child's head.

Pilgrim's Bonnet Materials

Pilgrim's Hat and Bonnet

Talk Like a Pilgrim

Work these old-fangled words into your conversations on Thanksgiving.

Bootless: Useless

Dally: To waste time

Done: Tired

Oh, Marry! Oh, no!

Toothsome: Delicious

Truly: Precisely or accurately

Roasted Fowl

Roasted Fowl

12- to 14-pound turkey
8 to 10 cups prepared stuffing
⅓ to ½ cup olive oil
Salt and pepper

Preheat the oven to 325°. Remove the turkey neck and giblets. Rinse the bird, both inside and out, with cold water and then pat dry. Place the turkey breast-side up on a rack in a roasting pan and loosely fill the neck and body cavity with the stuffing. Using skewers or a needle and kitchen twine, close the opening to the neck and the body cavity. Tie together the drumsticks and tuck the wings under the bird (your aim is to make sure that no part of the turkey sticks out). Coat the entire bird with olive oil and season with pepper and salt. Cover with aluminum foil and place the pan in the preheated oven.

The cooking time will vary, but count on about 20 minutes per pound, or about 4 to 4½ hours for a 12- to 14-pound bird. To ensure a moist turkey, baste every 30 minutes or so. Remove the foil with 1 hour to go, so that the bird will brown evenly. You'll know the turkey is ready when you prick the thigh and the juices run clear, or when you jiggle the drumsticks and they feel loose. When a meat thermometer is inserted in the thickest part of the thigh, the internal temperature should reach 180°. Let the bird sit for 20 minutes before carving. Serves 10 to 12.

Thanksgiving Menu

ABOUT THE FIRST harvest feast William Bradford wrote, "and besides waterfowl there was great store of wild turkeys, of which they took many." Thus turkey became the centerpiece for Thanksgiving. Serve it with stuffing, Dugout Canoes (below), mashed potatoes, and pumpkin pie.

Dugout Canoes

The Wampanoag made *mishoonash* (canoes) by carving out the insides of logs. Your kids can model this practice by scooping out the insides of zucchini to make vessels for Thanksgiving vegetables. Blanch the "canoes" in boiling water, then fill with frozen corn that's been cooked with a little cream and seasoned with salt and pepper. Finally, add "seats" cut out of carrots and "oars" made from peppers.

Can You Catch This?

rows, and each person holds hands with the player opposite her. The last pair forms an arch with their hands. Then the other players pass under the arch and reform the two rows. The game continues at least until everyone has had a chance to form the arch — but can continue endlessly. While playing, your mock Pilgrims can chant the following:

> *The needle's eye*
> *That doth supply*
> *The thread that*
> *Runs so true;*
> *Ah! many a lass*
> *Have I let past*
> *Because I wanted you.*

Miniature Cornucopias

For table party favors, fill sugar cones with fruit-shaped candies, marzipan fruits, candy corn, or fruit-shaped cereal, and tie with a ribbon.

Old-Fashioned Fun & Games

AFTER YOUR FEAST, challenge your guests to a round of games — 1621 style. **Can You Catch This?** Many Wampanoag games taught hand-eye coordination, which was crucial to mastering skills such as sewing and archery. To play this game of toss and catch, tie a 24-inch-long string 2 inches from the top of a 12-inch dowel. On the free end of the string, tie a loop about 3 inches in diameter. Hold the dowel in your hand with the stringed end pointing upward. Gently swing the string around and try to hook the loop onto the top of the dowel.

Thread the Needle: Best suited for younger children (of the "London Bridge Is Falling Down" age), this game takes its inspiration from the common seventeenth-century pastime of sewing. To play, several people stand in two

Holiday Cheer

Thread the Needle

Christmas Carnival

THE ENTHUSIASM that takes hold of kids from November to December makes them the perfect guests for a holiday celebration. Our gathering capitalizes on those high spirits with a round-robin of the season's best — quick crafts, silly games, and the merriest snacks this side of the North Pole.

PARTY STATS
Ages: All
Size: 8 to 20 guests
Length: 2 to 3 hours
Prep time: 3 hours
Cost: $4 to $6 per guest

Invitations

THIS SNAZZY Christmas tree collage makes a charming party invitation — but its real beauty lies in the fact that kids of all age groups, from toddlers to teens, can enjoy crafting it. Simply cut angled shapes from tissue paper, construction paper, leftover wrapping paper, or your children's recycled artwork, then glue them onto a picture of a tree on another piece of paper. Write the party details on the inside in green ink. You can either color-copy the invitation or handcraft one for each family.

Christmas Carnival Invitation

Deck the Halls

IN ADDITION to the tree (which is a party must), you and your kids can deck the halls, walls, and stairways with sprigs of holly and mistletoe, Christmas lights, and jingle bells. For a sweet wreath, tie an assortment of hard candies in their wrappers and a small pair of scissors to a ready-made wreath. As party guests arrive, they can snip off the sweets one at a time.

Sweet Wreath

Santa's Workshop

KEEP THE LITTLE elves busy at your party with one or two of the following holiday crafts.
Cardboard Gingerbread People: For a clever ornament, invite guests to decorate cardboard "cookies." To make one, trace a holiday cookie cutter on corrugated cardboard and cut with an X-Acto knife (a parent's job). Then invite the kids to decorate the cookies with puffy paint.
Holiday Garlands: Set out bowls of stringables — popcorn, beads, pinecones, buttons, or anything else that can be poked with a needle. Offer guests heavy-duty thread and let them dig into the bowls and string garlands.

Christmas Carnival

Christmas Carnival

Handy Tote

Handy Totes

Handy Totes: Let partygoers create a tote bag for hauling home all their party loot, from favors to holiday crafts. For best results, plan this activity early in the party before things get rollicking, and have kids work one at a time. Near a sink, cover your work surface with newspaper. Pour tempera paints in pie plates and have enough small paper bags with handles to go around. Offer each child a smock, then let her customize the front and back of a folded bag. Once dry, stuff the bag with party favors — candy canes, snow globes, ribbon candy, or homemade ornaments and garlands.

Gift Wrap: While you have the paint out, let kids craft gift wrap. Tape a sheet of newsprint or butcher paper onto a basement wall and let kids paint with handprints. Once dry, cut the paper into sections for each guest to take home.

Cheese Ball Snowman

This cheesy little guy is almost too cute to eat, but he makes a perky companion to a plate of crackers or mini bagels.

2 8-ounce packages cream cheese (for the head and body)
Raisins (eyes, mouth, buttons)
Piece of carrot (nose)
Crackers (hat)
Parsley sprig (optional, for hat)
Fruit leather (scarf)
Pretzels (arms)
Canned baby corn (pipe)
Toothpicks

From the cream cheese, fashion two balls for the head and body. (Note: Do not warm the cream cheese to room temperature.) Add face, buttons, hat, and scarf. Break pretzels and use the center sections for arms. Make the corncob pipe from half an ear of baby corn and a toothpick. Tip: For extra flavor, dress up the cream cheese with confectioners' sugar and lemon juice or feta cheese and garlic powder.

Reindeer Gear: Your crew can prance right into party mode by adorning themselves in the latest North Pole couture: easy-to-make reindeer antlers. Before the party, cut red poster board into 1½- by 24-inch-long strips for the headbands and cut brown poster board into 6- by 9-inch rectangles for the antlers (two for each child). Put out pencils, scissors, a stapler or two, glue and glitter, and, if you like, red face paint.

Help each guest wrap a strip around his or her head for a comfortable fit, remove it, and securely staple the ends. On the brown poster board, each child can outline a pair of multi-branched antlers and then cut them out. Kids who want spiffier antlers can add glue and glitter; less patient reindeer can just staple the antlers to the front of the headband. Use face paint to finish off each reindeer's costume with a big red nose.

Crudi-tree

This make-ahead centerpiece is not only spectacular to look at, but it's also a tower of healthy, sugar-free nibbling. Start with a 12-inch, green Styrofoam cone and use toothpicks to attach vegetables (broccoli florets, cucumber slices, olives, sugar snap peas, cherry tomatoes, and sliced red, yellow, and green peppers). Top the tree with a yellow pepper star. Serve with your favorite vegetable dip. Tip: Be careful using the toothpicks — try pressing them in with a thimble. Also, don't worry about covering every inch of the cone at first. Go back later and stuff bits of broccoli (without toothpicks) into the bare spots.

Reindeer Gear

Christmas Carnival

Tree-sicles

These treats are made with your favorite sugar cookie dough. Roll the dough to a ⅛-inch thickness and cut with tree-shaped cookie cutters. Sandwich a craft stick between two cookies and bake as usual. (Note: The cookies are thick, so baking may take longer.) Cool and frost with green frosting, then add icing, candy, and sprinkles. Tip: Separate the decorating goodies into cupcake holders and give each child his own assortment to use.

The Reindeer Games

ONCE YOUR GANG has finished making crafts, it's time for silly games and contests of skill (and the chance to score a few prizes). The following events include several that kids like to play over and over, plus a few one-timers that work best with the whole group. Before the big day, be sure to lay in a supply of inexpensive prizes, such as candy canes, stickers, marbles, and rubber balls.

Snowblowers: A good set of lungs and coolness under pressure are essential for this contest. To set up, tape large paper cups to one side of a table so that the cup openings are level with the table's surface. Fill each cup halfway with small prizes (candy canes, colored pencils, stickers, bright erasers) and clear away any chairs so players have an open pathway at both sides of the table. Give the first two players paper towel tubes and explain that when you place a Ping-Pong ball in front of each of them, they must blow through the tubes like a snowblower. (Point out that a gentle breath is all it takes to get the "snowball" rolling.) Each contestant will have 15 seconds to direct the ball across the table and into one of the paper cups; if the ball goes over the edge first, that player's turn is over. Each winner gets to pick one prize from the cup — and the playing continues until each cup is empty.

Stuff the Santa: This merry game pits teams against one another in a race to create the stoutest Saint Nick of them all. To play, you and your kids will need to inflate an ample supply of balloons and borrow or buy a red, one-piece union suit in Santa's size — extra large.

Contestants are divided into teams of four to six players. Draw candy canes to determine which player will don the suit over his or her clothes; the player selecting the longest candy cane is "Santa." Teammates are given the task

Snowblowers

Stuff the Santa

of stuffing the suit with balloons. Remind the players that a gentle touch is essential for keeping balloons intact. Set a timer for 2 minutes and see how many balloons the team can stuff into the suit before the time is up. The next team of Santa stuffers must try to top the previous record, but first give old Santa a chance to show off his lumpy physique.

Full of Beans: Pique your guests' curiosity with this classic puzzler: How many red and green jelly beans are in the glass jar? During the party, each contestant must write his or her name and best estimate on a slip of paper and drop it into a box with everyone else's guesses. At the end of the party, read off each estimate and record it on a large sheet of paper. Then, with great flourish, pull out a sealed envelope with the answer in it and announce the correct number. The

winner is the person (or persons, in the case of a tie) whose guess comes the closest. For the brilliant deduction, the winner takes home the candy jar and its contents.

Full of Beans

Cookie Swap

For an easy holiday party, invite guests to a cookie swap. Karla Davison of Fairfax, Virginia, had her sons deliver invitations to nearby friends, asking them to make two dozen cookies for party day. Karla then displayed the cookies at her house and had each child talk about his or her contribution. After games and crafts, everyone chowed down — and took a bag of cookies home to share with Mom and Dad.

Hanukkah Party

PARTY STATS

Ages: All
Size: 8 to 20 guests
Length: 2 hours
Prep time: 1 hour
Cost: $1 per guest

EVERY HANUKKAH, the Wallace family of Saratoga, California, brightens up their home with a Festival of Lights party. The premise is simple: friends and family are invited to bring a menorah and share in the lighting together. Barbara, the mother of two boys, says, "To have our home filled with all of these menorahs, especially the ones that hold memories, is a wonderful way to celebrate the holiday.

Hanukkah Hand Invitations

TO MAKE A MENORAH invitation, trace both of your child's hands onto blue paper, overlapping the thumbs to make the shammes candle in the middle. Next glue the paper cut-out onto a sheet of white paper folded in half. Light up the flames with a gold glitter crayon. Write the party details inside the card, including a request that guests bring their own menorah to light. Anything goes, whether it's a menorah made at Hebrew school or a great grandmother's prize menorah.

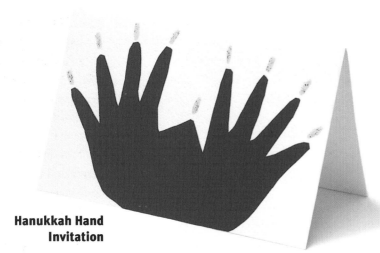

Hanukkah Hand Invitation

Lighting the Menorah

THE MAIN EVENT at the Wallaces' party is when everyone illuminates the menorahs. They light them at the kitchen table (draped with a nonflammable tablecloth), then put one menorah in the dining room windowsill, one at the kids' table, and the rest all around the house.

With so many menorahs, all of the kids get the chance to light a candle. "There's something magical about lighting the candles, especially for kids," says Barb.

Playing Dreidel

INVITE GUESTS to spin the dreidel — and try to take home the pot. Explain that the dreidel top is decorated with the first four letters from the Hebrew phrase *Nes gadol hayah sham*, which means "A great miracle happened there." To play this game of chance, everybody begins with an equal amount of chocolates, coins, or peanuts. Before each round, players ante up. The players spin and follow directions based on the letter that's faceup when the dreidel stops:

נ (nun) — take nothing from the pot
ג (gimel) — take the whole pot
ה (hay) — take half the pot
שׁ (shin) — add two items to the pot

You can play for a set number of rounds or until someone has won everything.

Chocolate Menorah

Playing Dreidel

BRIGHTEN — and sweeten — your family's Hanukkah celebration with this double-chocolate menorah.

1¼ cups semisweet chocolate chips
½ cup white chocolate morsels
⅓ cup heavy cream

Melt ¼ cup of the semisweet chocolate chips in a microwave-safe bowl, about 1 minute on high. Using a clean paintbrush, drizzle the chocolate on the inside of one regular and eight mini foil muffin cups. Next melt the white chocolate morsels in the microwave and paint over the drizzled chocolate. Place the mini cups in a mini-muffin pan and the large muffin cup in a custard cup. Freeze for 5 to 10 minutes, or until hardened.

Meanwhile, make the ganache filling. Heat the heavy cream in the microwave until it comes to a boil, then stir in 1 cup of chocolate chips until melted and smooth. Spoon the ganache into the candy cups. Refrigerate for 1 hour, or until set. To assemble the menorah, place the candy cups on a large platter or board with the largest cup in the center. Insert candles into each cup, then light in the traditional manner. Serves 9.

Week of Guests

In Santa Fe, New Mexico, *Family Fun* reader Miriam Sagan's family celebrates Hanukkah with the traditional rituals — lighting the menorah, frying latkes, and giving gifts. They also follow an old European custom of inviting a mix of people to their house every night of the holiday. Word gets around, so when one of their guests can't make it, someone else is sure to call and say, "Hey, we heard you need people on night number six, and we're volunteering!"

Party Resources

Party Locations

For a change of pace from the home party, consider taking the kids out. Not only will an alternative setting spare wear and tear on your home (and your nerves), but the kids will have a blast, too. Once you've settled on a location, call and find out if they offer party packages or group discounts. Here are some locations to consider:

◆ Bowling alley
◆ Ice or roller skating rink
◆ Radio, television, fire, or police station
◆ Pizza parlor or local restaurant
◆ Planetarium
◆ Ceramics studio
◆ Children's museum
◆ Farm
◆ Circus, zoo, or aquarium
◆ Kids' gymnastics or sports center
◆ Movie or theater matinee
◆ Nature center
◆ Miniature golf or batting center
◆ Playground
◆ Basketball court or baseball field
◆ Local park or pool
◆ Beauty parlor
◆ Water or theme park

Party Supplies

Birthday Express
11220 120th Avenue NE
Kirkland, WA 98033-4535
1-800-4-BIRTHDAY
www.birthdayexpress.com
For busy parents, this mail-order (and online) catalog is a real time-saver. You can purchase complete party packages, from the invitations to the favors, for popular children's party themes, such as Thomas the Tank Engine, Madeline, and Winnie the Pooh. Call, write, or e-mail for a free catalog.

M&N International, Inc.
P.O. Box 64784
St. Paul, MN 55164
800-479-2043
This 200-page mail-order catalog features hundreds of party decorations and accessories for every holiday of the year, from the back-to-school season to Fourth of July. Call for a free catalog.

MeadowLark Party Shoppe
2 Beistle Plaza
Meadowlands Mall
Shippensburg, PA 17257
717-532-3535
www.cvn.net/meadowlands/pshoppe.htm
MeadowLark, a mail-order party supply company, specializes in theme decorations and party kits with over 13,000 items to choose from. Visit their outlet store in Shippensburg, Pennsylvania, or call, write, or e-mail to order the $7.85 catalog (which includes a 25% off coupon).

Party and Paper Retailer Magazine
www.partypaper.com
If you're looking to find a party store in your area, check out this online resource. Click on your state in the retail locator for a handy listing.

Party and Paper Worldwide
www.partypro.com
Shop in this online party supply store as if you were shopping in a super party warehouse for "Birthday in a box" packages, piñatas, paper supplies, and much more.

Party Favors

Oriental Trading Company, Inc.
P.O. Box 3407
Omaha, NE 68103
1-800-327-9678
www.oriental.com
This 100-page mail-order catalog is overflowing with party favors, prizes, and gifts for children's birthday and holiday parties. Many of the items can be ordered in bulk. Write or call for a free catalog.

The Nature Company
www.naturecompany.com
1-800-447-8828
This retail chain offers a selection of nature-themed toys and favors, such as tumbled rocks, rubber balls, spyglasses and magnifiers, tops, and plastic animals. Call or use the online store locator to find a store in your area.

MediBadge, Inc.
P.O. Box 12456
Omaha, NE 68112
800-228-0040
www.medibadge.com
If you're looking to fill a treasure chest with favors, stickers, erasers, and tiny plastic toys, check out this mail-order catalog. MediBadge supplies children's novelties in bulk to medical and dental offices — and to the public. Call for a free catalog.

Zany Brainy
888-WOW-KIDS
www.zanybrainy.com
Zany Brainy specializes in educational toys for kids, but they also carry stickers, rubber stamps, science favors, children's books, and craft supplies. Call or e-mail to locate a store in your area, or to order a free catalog.

Cake and Candy Resources

Wilton Enterprises
2240 W. 75th Street
Woodridge, IL 60517
800-772-7111

Wilton is the ultimate source for all your cake decorating needs, from novelty cake pans and cookie cutters to food coloring paste and cake decorations. Call or write for the $7.99 catalog, or to find a local distributor.

King Arthur Flour
P.O. Box 1010, Route 5 South
Norwich, VT 05055
800-777-4434
www.kingarthurflour.com
This mail-order catalog features unbleached flours, baking pans and supplies, colored sugars and sprinkles, marzipan, and cake decorating tools. Call for a free catalog or visit their retail store in Norwich, Vermont.

Sugarcraft
1143 South Erie Boulevard
Hamilton, OH 45011
513-896-7089
www.sugarcraft.com
This online cake decorating, cookie making, and candy supply catalog features over 10,000 items, from cake pans and candy molds to sugar flowers and edible images. Order items online or visit their retail store in Hamilton, Ohio.

Sweet Expectations
8 Crafts Avenue
Northampton, MA 01060
413-585-8965
www.sweet-expectations.com
An old-fashioned candy store in *FamilyFun*'s hometown that stocks many of the candies featured on our cake designs. Call for a price list or to order hard-to-find candies, or visit the store in Northampton, Massachusetts.

Rental Sources

American Rental Association
www.ararental.org/consumermain.htm
If you're short on plates, tables, and chairs, or you'd like to rent a moonwalk or cotton candy maker, head to a rental store in your area. To find one, simply enter your zipcode in this online search engine.

Taylor Rental, Grand Rental Station, or TruServ
www.taylorrentals.com
This national rental company has over 600 retail stores in the United States. Check the Yellow Pages under "rental service" or search the online guide to find addresses and phone numbers of rental stores in your area.

Rental Prices

If you'd like to add punch to your block parties or large gatherings, consider renting any of the following items. To find a rental store in your area, see the sources at left (prices may vary).

◆ Helium tank: $10 to $25
◆ Karaoke: $45 to $60
◆ Bubble maker: $20 to $30
◆ Fog maker: $10 to $50
◆ PA lectern: $30
◆ Chairs: $.65 to $2 each
◆ Tables: $4.50 to $20 each
◆ Table settings: $.30 to $.50 per piece
◆ Moonwalk: $75 to $140
◆ Popcorn cart: $30 to $45
◆ Snowcone maker: $35
◆ Cotton candy machine: $40 to $50
◆ Grill: $35 to $85
◆ Dunk tank: $100 to $200

Hiring Party Entertainers

An entertainer, whether he's a magician or a clown, can add an exciting element to a birthday or holiday party. To find one in your area, check the Yellow Pages under "entertainers," or read or post ads in the newspaper and on library bulletin boards.

Once you have someone in mind, set up an interview. Ask him or her what the show includes and the approximate duration of their act. You may also wish to see a videotape of a performance or request references.

The following is a list of entertainers you might consider hiring for your party (review it with your kids).

◆ Police officer or firefighter (call the station for information; some firefighters or police officers may be willing to bring their vehicles)
◆ Disc jockey
◆ Musician
◆ Naturalist (with animal friends)
◆ Clown
◆ Magician
◆ Storyteller
◆ Puppeteer
◆ Costumed character
◆ Farmer who offers pony rides
◆ Mad scientist
◆ Ballerinas
◆ Game coordinator

Index

Art & Photography Credits

Special thanks to the following *FamilyFun* magazine photographers, illustrators, and stylists for their excellent work.

PHOTOGRAPHERS:

Jean Mitchell Allsop: *47 (3 bottom)*

Jade Albert: *Cover*

Robert Benson: *6 (top), 7 (middle left), 30 (middle & bottom left) 31-33, 58, 59 (bottom), 60, 61 (bottom, middle & top left), 174, 195, 198 (bottom left), 199 (top right)*

Paul Berg: *111 (top left), 160 (bottom left), 161, 162, 213 (bottom right)*

Robert Bossi: *100, 132 (bottom), 133 (top right), 134-143*

Michael Carroll: *150 (bottom left), 151, 196 (bottom right), 197, 198 (top right & middle left)*

Alma D. Derungs: *165 (right)*

Faith Echtermeyer: *68 (bottom left & middle)*

Alan Epstein: *81 (middle & bottom), 82 (bottom)*

Peter Fox: *62 (bottom left), 84 (bottom), 109, 110, 119, 182 (bottom left and top left), back cover (top right), 206 (bottom left)*

Jim Gipe: *10 (bottom right), 17, 206 (middle right), 212 (bottom)*

Thomas Heinser: *6 (middle right), 123-125, 126 (bottom & top right), 127, back cover (middle)*

Tom Hopkins: *7 (top left), 22, 24, 42 (bottom & middle right), 43, 45, 50 (bottom right & top left), 51, 53 (middle & bottom right), 54, 55 (bottom and top right), 87,*

88 (bottom left), 89 (top middle), 101 (left and right bottom), 102-104, 105 (top right & bottom left), 106, 107 (top right), 129, 130, 149 (top left), 155, 156 (bottom), 157-159, 164 (bottom), 165 (top), 166, 206 (top right & 2 middle right), 207-211, back cover (top left, bottom left & bottom right)

Ed Judice: *6 (bottom left, middle right, top left & right corner), 7 (bottom right & middle left), 19, 36 (bottom), 41 (2 bottom left), 44, 46 (middle), 49, 52, 55, (2 top left), 57, 71 (top left), 73, 77 (bottom right), 79 (middle & top right), 85 (middle right & 2 bottom), 86 (2 middle right), 88 (middle right), 90 (bottom left), 92, 95 (bottom left), 121 (2 bottom right), 133 (bottom right), 154 (middle left), 160 (middle right), 172, 180, 181 (middle & bottom left), 182 (middle), 183 (top & bottom right), 194 (2 bottom & 1 top right), 196 (bottom, right side, middle left & top), 206 (bottom left), 223, back cover (middle left)*

Michael Kevin/The Stock Market: *212 (middle right)*

Ed Kohn: *163 (bottom)*

Rob Lang: *84 (top left)*

Brian Leatart: *46 (bottom right), 111 (bottom right), 167 (bottom right), 188 (bottom), 189-192, 193 (top middle)*

Lightworks Photographic: *18 (middle), 36 (middle & middle right), 148 (bottom), 163 (top), 183 (bottom left), 188 (2 top right), 205 (right top)*

Dorit Lombroso: *80, 82 (top right)*

Dave Madison/Tony Stone Images: *83*

Marcy Malloy: *74, 91 (middle), 93*

Tom McWilliam: *6 (middle left & bottom right), 7 (middle right), 8, 25 (middle & bottom right), 26, 27 (middle right & bottom left), 28 (middle right & bottom left), 29 (top left & right), 34 (3 bottom left), 35, 37, 39, 40 (bottom), 41 (top left & bottom), 56 (bottom left), 62 (middle right), 63 (bottom right), 66 (bottom left & middle), 67, 69 (bottom right) 70, (bottom left), 71 (bottom), 72 (bottom left), 76, 94 (bottom left), 95 (top right), 96, 97 (top left), 144, 146, 147 (bottom right), 149 (bottom right), 152, 153, 154 (top and bottom right), 155, 168-171, 175 (bottom), 176, 177 (top right), 178 (bottom right), 179 (top left), 200-204, 205 (top left, bottom right & middle left), back cover (middle right)*

Doug Menuez: *98, 112 (bottom left), 113-117*

Russell Photography: *78 (middle left), 118 (bottom left), 194 (middle)*

Jim Scherer: *9, 48 (bottom), 64 (bottom)*

Joanne Schmaltz: *41 (right), 75, 79 (middle left), 85 (top right), 97 (2 bottom right)*

Shaffer/Smith: *2, 3 (top), 7 (top right), 10 (top middle & bottom), 11-13, 15 (bottom left, bottom right & top), 16 (bottom left), 18, 20, 21, 23, 27 (top right), 29 (bottom right) 38, 47 (top left), 56 (2 middle), 63 (3 top), 65 (middle & bottom right), 69 (top left), 71 (bottom right), 82 (3 middle), 90 (middle right), 99, 107 (bottom left & middle left), 108, 118 (middle), 122, 128, 131 (bottom), 145, 148 (top left), 167 (top), 173, 177 (bottom left), 178 (top left), 179 (bottom right), 184-187, 193 (bottom right), 199 (bottom right), 213 (top), 224 (top), back cover (middle right) and balloons on the opening page of each party and balloons on the cover*

Luigart/Stayner: *15 (bottom)*

Steve Smith: *120*

Jake Wyman: *213 (bottom)*

ILLUSTRATORS:

Doug Bantz: *89*

Paul Meisel: *78*

David Sales: *72 (top right)*

STYLISTS:

Kimberly Amussen/Team, Bonnie Anderson/Team, Grace Arias, Melissa Boudreau/Team, Catherine Callahan, D.J. Carey, Carol Cole, Pamela Courtleigh, Bill Doggett, Katia Echivard, Erica Ell/Team, Susan Fox, Ron Garcia, Karen Gillingham, Harriet Granthem, Elaine Greenstein, Sue Grunweld, Jennifer Hanna, Karen Lidbeck, Marie Piraino, Sally-Jo O'brien, George Simone, Edwina Stevenson

Painting Party, page 71

Also from FamilyFun magazine

★ **FamilyFun magazine:** a creative guide to all the great things families can do together. Call 800-289-4849 for a subscription.

★ **FamilyFun's Cookbook** by Deanna F. Cook and the experts at *FamilyFun* magazine: a collection of more than 500 irresistible recipes for you and your kids, from healthy snacks to birthday cakes to dinners everyone in the family can enjoy.

★ **FamilyFun's Crafts** by Deanna F. Cook and the experts at *FamilyFun* magazine: a step-by-step guide to more than 500 of the best crafts and activities to do with your kids.

★ **FamilyFun's Games on the Go** by Lisa Stiepock and the experts at *FamilyFun* magazine: a roundup of 250 great games and tips for families traveling by car, plane, or train.

★ **FamilyFun's Cookies for Christmas** by Deanna F. Cook and the experts at *FamilyFun* magazine: a batch of 50 recipes for creative holiday treats.

★ **FamilyFun.com:** visit us at http://www.familyfun.com and search for articles, post messages, and e-mail editors.